Student Matters

ISSUES

Volume 185

Series Editor

Lisa Firth

Independence

Educational Publishers
Cambridge

First published by Independence
The Studio, High Green
Great Shelford
Cambridge CB22 5EG
England

© Independence 2010

British Library Cataloguing in Publication Data
Student Matters — (Issues; v.185)
1. Education, Higher — Great Britain 2. Education,
Higher — Standards — Great Britain 3. Higher education and
state — Great Britain
I. Series II. Firth, Lisa
378.4'1-dc22

ISBN-13: 978 1 86168 526 1

Printed in Great Britain
MWL Print Group Ltd

Cover
The illustration on the front cover is by
Don Hatcher.

CONTENTS

Chapter One: Student Issues

Chapter Two: University Standards

Chapter Three: Graduate Prospects

Useful information for readers

Dear Reader,

Issues: Student Matters

More young people are going into higher education now than ever before. Meanwhile, the debate about university standards continues to rage. Are degrees still valuable to modern employers? Is university too expensive? Is the graduate job market saturated? Does a university education boost social mobility? Is the higher education system elitist? These are just some of the questions debated in **Student Matters**.

The purpose of *Issues*

Student Matters is the one hundred and eighty-fifth volume in the **Issues** series. The aim of this series is to offer up-to-date information about important issues in our world. Whether you are a regular reader or new to the series, we do hope you find this book a useful overview of the many and complex issues involved in the topic.

Titles in the **Issues** series are resource books designed to be of especial use to those undertaking project work or requiring an overview of facts, opinions and information on a particular subject, particularly as a prelude to undertaking their own research.

The information in this book is not from a single author, publication or organisation; the value of this unique series lies in the fact that it presents information from a wide variety of sources, including:
⇨ Government reports and statistics
⇨ Newspaper articles and features
⇨ Information from think-tanks and policy institutes
⇨ Magazine features and surveys
⇨ Website material
⇨ Literature from lobby groups and charitable organisations. *

Critical evaluation

Because the information reprinted here is from a number of different sources, readers should bear in mind the origin of the text and whether the source is likely to have a particular bias or agenda when presenting information (just as they would if undertaking their own research). It is hoped that, as you read about the many aspects of the issues explored in this book, you will critically evaluate the information presented. It is important that you decide whether you are being presented with facts or opinions. Does the writer give a biased or an unbiased report? If an opinion is being expressed, do you agree with the writer?

Student Matters offers a useful starting point for those who need convenient access to information about the many issues involved. However, it is only a starting point. Following each article is a URL to the relevant organisation's website, which you may wish to visit for further information.

Kind regards,

Lisa Firth
Editor, **Issues** series

** Please note that Independence Publishers has no political affiliations or opinions on the topics covered in the **Issues** series, and any views quoted in this book are not necessarily those of the publisher or its staff.*

ISSUES TODAY
A RESOURCE FOR KEY STAGE 3

Younger readers can also benefit from the thorough editorial process which characterises the **Issues** series with our resource books for 11- to 14-year-old students, **Issues Today**. In addition to containing information from a wide range of sources, rewritten with this age group in mind, **Issues Today** titles also feature comprehensive glossaries, an accessible and attractive layout and handy tasks and assignments which can be used in class, for homework or as a revision aid. In addition, these titles are fully photocopiable. For more information, please visit our website (www.independence. co.uk).

The benefits of higher education

Higher education could boost your career prospects and earning potential, while giving you the chance to immerse yourself in a subject that really interests you – and get involved in lots of other activities

Is higher education right for you?

Higher education is about taking your education to the next level: learning new things and getting to where you want to be.

A higher education qualification could help you take charge of your future by building skills and confidence and opening up new opportunities – whatever stage of life you're at. Even if no one else you know is thinking about going into higher education, it could still be the right choice for you.

There are currently over two million higher education students in the UK

There are currently over two million higher education students in the UK. Higher education courses are offered at around 130 universities and higher education colleges, and many further education colleges.

With more than 50,000 courses in a variety of academic and work-related subjects – including many that let you combine more than one subject – there's bound to be one that suits you.

Why go to university or college?

Higher education could benefit you in a number of ways. University or college lets you experience a rich cultural and social scene, meeting a variety of people while studying something you love.

A higher education qualification can also lead to increased earning potential, a wider range of opportunities and a more rewarding career. Many employers target graduates in their recruitment campaigns.

And on average, graduates tend to earn substantially more than people with A-levels who did not go to university. Projected over a working lifetime, the difference is something like £100,000 before tax at today's valuation.

What can you study?

Higher education courses range from familiar academic subjects such as English or history, less familiar ones such as philosophy, and a host of work-related (vocational) courses such as accountancy.

Higher education doesn't necessarily mean getting an honours degree – you could study a foundation degree, a Higher National Certificate (HNC) or Higher National Diploma (HND), or a Diploma of Higher Education.

Many courses are based on units of study or 'modules'. Each module lets you earn credits towards your qualification, while giving you a degree of flexibility over the focus of your studies.

How much will it cost?

The costs of being a student vary between different parts of the UK – and so can the length of courses. Financial support is available, so money needn't be a barrier. The help you can get depends on your family situation and the type of course you're doing.

⇨ The above information is reprinted with kind permission from Directgov. Visit www.direct.gov.uk for more.
© Crown copyright

Going to university

Student life doesn't just offer higher education. It's also an opportunity to learn first-class financial management skills that will last you for life. The good news is that help about money is available to anybody thinking about going to university

Student loans

Student loans can take a large burden off the cost of going to university. You won't need to repay the loan until you've finished your studies and are earning enough to do so.

You can apply for a loan that will just cover the cost of tuition fees, or for a larger one that will contribute to your living expenses as well. The Student Loans Company can give advice about the type of loan to suit you.

Grants and allowances

Depending on your financial circumstances (taking into account your family's household income), you may be eligible for a Maintenance Grant or Special Support Grant. This will contribute towards accommodation and other living costs, and won't need to be paid back.

Extra allowances are also available for people with disabilities (including specific learning difficulties) as well as for students who have children or adult dependants.

Bursaries, scholarships and awards

Your university or college can offer extra financial help in the form of a bursary. This might be an amount paid directly to your bank account, or a discount on your accommodation costs. Publicly funded universities charging full tuition fees must give you a bursary if you receive the full Maintenance Grant or Special Support Grant.

Many universities, colleges, charities and educational trusts offer different types of scholarships and awards. These can be awarded for exceptional talents or academic achievements, and the amount may be based on your household income. It's worth asking your university or college what's available to apply for.

You don't have to pay money back from a bursary, scholarship or award.

Access to Learning Fund

If you're in hardship and need extra support to fund student life, the Access to Learning Fund may help. Provided through your university or college, this will take into account your individual circumstances. It will assess whether you need financial support for costs not already covered by other grants. These costs could include childcare, support over vacation periods if friends and family cannot help, and emergency costs such as essential household repairs.

How else can you fund your studies?

You may be lucky enough to receive cash from your parents. An alternative way to boost your bank balance, as well as your CV, is to get a part-time job. This could fit around your term-time schedule of studying and socialising, or you could do full-time temporary work during the holidays.

Do your research on different types of student bank accounts before settling on one that best suits your finances in the long term

Bank on it

Many high-street banks will try to attract students with free overdrafts, special offers and discounts on shops and services. Do your research on different types of student bank accounts before settling on one that best suits your finances in the

long term. For example, an account charging a lower Annual Percentage Rate (APR) on loans may be better overall than those offering gimmicks during freshers' week.

Do the sums

The cost of student life soon mounts up, so it's important to estimate your expenses before deciding on where to study and live. Doing the sums will help you decide what type of financial support to apply for.

Here are some areas to budget for:

⇨ Tuition fees: You usually pay these in one or more instalments. If you need help to pay them, contact your local education authority for advice.

⇨ Household costs: How much you pay will depend on location and the type of digs you choose. Halls of residence usually charge an all-inclusive fee that covers rent, cleaning, electricity, etc. and also some of your meals. Alternatively, you might decide to live in a shared flat where each tenant pays a fair share towards the cost of rent and bills. As a full-time student you will be eligible either for a discount on, or exemption from, council tax.

⇨ Study essentials: Textbooks, stationery, computer equipment and photocopying all come at a price, but keep an eye out for special discounts offered by retail outlets, especially at the beginning of the autumn term. Also, find out whether your university offers free or subsidised photocopying and equipment.

⇨ Travel: Take into account the cost of travelling around town or visiting family and friends. If you travel by train, think about investing in a Young Person's Railcard to benefit from fare discounts. If you're travelling abroad, it's a good idea to get an International Student Identity Card (ISIC), which entitles you to thousands of discounts worldwide.

⇨ Living costs: We're talking groceries, clothes, mobile phones and everything else you couldn't live without. You may be entitled to help towards healthcare costs, such as prescription charges, eye tests and dental checks, so ask your student union or healthcare centre.

Set aside some money for nights out on the town, and remember that many places offer discounts to students with an NUS card. *This Life Stage Guide has been provided by TheSite.org – your guide to the real world.*

Tips

'You feel that everything that's coming in, whether it's a loan, your wages, or a loan off your parents, it always seems to go straight towards the uni, or a fee or a book. Or if you are going out socialising, you do have to socialise when you're at uni, then it's all going to the same sort of place.'
Joanna, 20, student, Birmingham

'During August and September time you're sorting yourself out, where you're going, what course you're on, things like that, you start seeing TV and newspapers bombarding you with student accounts all offering you things.'
Jane, 21, student, Birmingham

⇨ The above information is reprinted with kind permission from TheSite.org. Visit www.thesite.org for more information.

© *TheSite.org*

What is higher education really like?

Higher education means a lot more than just getting a qualification. It also offers you the chance to meet new people and take advantage of new opportunities

What is higher education all about?

Unlike school, you're at university or college because you want to be, learning more about a subject or job you're really into. You'll have more control over how and when you study – though it's up to you to make the most of it.

You'll find higher education challenging – getting used to new ways of learning and thinking may take time – but you'll have a lot of fun along the way. You'll also have lots of opportunities to experience new things and meet new people.

What you can study

You can study lots of interesting subjects at university or a college offering higher education courses. Most people study one or two subjects, but in a lot of detail.

There are higher education courses in subjects you studied at school, like maths or English. Or there are more unusual options, such as criminology (the study of crime) or software engineering (learning to write computer software – games or other programs). Other courses lead to a specific job: for example, journalism or medicine.

It's possible to study 'combined' courses. For example, someone wishing to follow a career in politics but with an interest in art might study both subjects together.

Studying and social life

Studying

Higher education is a very different experience to school or further education.

You are expected to do far more work for yourself. Lectures and seminars will provide guidance, but you'll need to widen your knowledge through background reading.

Subject staff will offer lots of advice to help you get used to this new way of working. Library staff will be able to help you find the materials you need, and advise on referencing and avoiding plagiarism when it comes to writing essays.

Socialising

Making new friends is a key part of the higher education experience. If you're worried about fitting in, remember that students from all backgrounds and of all ages go to university and college.

One way to form friendships is through student societies or sports. It's always easier to bond with someone if you share a common interest. There will probably be a full list of societies available on your students' union website, and you'll have an opportunity to join up to most at the 'freshers' fair'.

Most institutions have a sports centre of their own or an arrangement with the local centre. As a student you're likely to have access to sports facilities, and you may get a discount on gym membership.

Getting a taste of student life

Most universities and colleges run open days. They're generally held two or three times a year, allowing members of the public to look around the institution and see what's on offer. Many institutions also offer short courses over the summer period, giving prospective students the chance to get a taste of higher education.

At these events you'll be able to find out from lecturers and students all the good and bad points of university life, take a tour of the campus and sit in on lectures and seminars.

UNIAID's online games are another way of getting a handle on what day-to-day life as a student is really like. By taking you through a term as a virtual student, they may well raise some issues you hadn't even considered.

⇨ The above information is reprinted with kind permission from Directgov. Visit www.direct.gov.uk for more.
© *Crown copyright*

High levels of satisfaction among students

National Student Survey shows increased participation and continued high levels of satisfaction among higher education students

Numbers of respondents to higher education's (HE) National Student Survey (NSS) were up this year, and four-fifths of students expressed satisfaction with the course they did.

The total number of students who responded to the fifth annual NSS increased this year by over 3,000 to 223,363 students; this gives an overall response rate for the UK of 62 per cent. A total of 155 higher education institutions (HEIs) across the UK and 117 further education colleges (FECs) in England took part.

The survey shows that the overall satisfaction rate (Question 22 in the survey) for students studying HE in England remains high: 81 per cent said that they are satisfied with their course.

For the first time this year students studying NHS subjects were able to respond to the survey by phone and post, in addition to the online survey they have used in previous years. This change has meant an increase in the overall response rate from this group from 37 per cent last year, to 65 per cent this year.

This is the second year that students studying HE courses at English FECs have participated in the survey. Their overall satisfaction is 75 per cent, with participation in the NSS at 57 per cent.

---

81 per cent of students surveyed said that they are satisfied with their course

---

HEFCE Chief Executive, Sir Alan Langlands, said:

'The increase in participation and the continued high levels of satisfaction in this year's NSS results demonstrate the commitment of institutions to deliver learning and teaching which is meeting the needs of their students. In the coming months it will be important for institutions to look closely at the results and identify

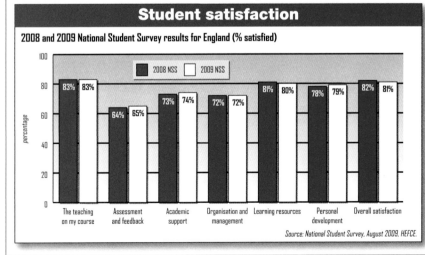

Student satisfaction

2008 and 2009 National Student Survey results for England (% satisfied)

Source: National Student Survey, August 2009, HEFCE.

areas where improvements can be made.'

David Lammy, Minister of State for Higher Education, said:

'High quality teaching is essential for a strong university sector, and it has never been more so than in the current climate where we want to ensure that students have the skills they need to progress and build up the UK's economy.

'Once again we are seeing students that are very satisfied, with over 80 per cent consistently rating their teaching experience highly. Five years of these high rates demonstrates that our higher education system is continuing to meet the challenge of providing a rewarding and quality experience to students across the country.'

Professor Paul Ramsden, CEO, Higher Education Academy, said:

'A high-quality student experience is the hallmark of excellent higher education. With the current pressures on the sector, it is striking that the vast majority of students are positive about the teaching they receive and about their experiences generally. It's a tribute to the commitment of everyone who works in higher education, but it makes it even more important that we keep our eyes on the ball and continue to deliver really good teaching for all students.'

Professor Janet Beer, chair of the NSS steering group and Vice-Chancellor of Oxford Brookes University, said:

'The increase in participation and continuing high levels of satisfaction demonstrate that students are engaging seriously with the survey as an important means by which to maintain and enhance the quality of their experience. There is a particularly pleasing upward trend in the percentage of students satisfied with the processes of assessment and feedback. This is an area in which universities are constantly – in partnership with their students – striving for improvement.'

Wes Streeting, President of the NUS, said:

'We are pleased that most students remain happy with the quality of university courses. However, we are concerned that the survey reveals a small dip in overall levels of satisfaction as the first group of students to pay top-up fees prepared to graduate. There is clearly no room for complacency on the part of universities, who have a responsibility to improve standards in accordance with their increased resources.'
6 August 2009

⇨ The above information is reprinted with kind permission from HEFCE. Visit www.hefce.ac.uk for more information. To search, review and compare subjects at universities and colleges in the UK visit Unistats.com. This site includes the results of the annual NSS.

© HEFCE

Choosing a course

Information from InterStudent

So, the UCAS deadline is fast approaching. You know the benefits of a university education, but you just can't decide what to do. After all, there are tens of thousands of courses (which is liberating if a little scary). Now is a good time to remember that you're no longer going to be tied to the school or college curriculum and to realise that there is a huge variety of subjects out there for you to choose from.

Even degrees with the same name can be radically different at different institutions

Maybe you're passionate about your A-level art course and are determined to carry it on to university. There are currently more than 3,000 different art courses alone, so there are ways of doing art that you probably haven't even imagined yet.

On the other hand, maybe you're tempted by the thought of something completely different? Even if you opt for something relatively obscure, such as a course in Korean, there are more than 20 courses available. If you want to be seriously obscure why not try Akkadian (an ancient Language and Empire), for which there were only two courses available.

The other thing to remember is that even degrees with the same name can be radically different at different institutions – from the syllabus and teaching style to the balance of exams and continuous assessment. The tens of thousands of courses are starting to look like an underestimate.

At this point a pin and a long list is not going to get you very far and you will have to do some research into the courses, and how different universities and colleges teach them. There are plenty of ways you can do this: read the prospectus and the student alternative guides (free from the university or from the students' union – just call or email and ask), read websites like InterStudent or books covering the same subject, visit the university and talk to tutors and students, talk to your teachers and to your parents, check out the department on the Internet. Treat all the information as you would any other sales literature (and remember that that is all it is) and be prepared to ask questions before you commit yourself.

Undoubtedly you probably want a good job after graduating and this will have an influence on your choice of institution. Check the employment rates for the graduates for a course but remember these can be misleading – the question of what sort of jobs they get is something to probe when you make contact with admissions staff or at an open day. They may well just be flipping burgers – a slight waste of three years of American Studies (or maybe not if you've seen the American love of burgers first hand!). So, once again, beware the sales talk – and remember that doing a law degree isn't necessarily the best way into a big city law firm (they might prefer someone who had studied Akkadian and then done legal training). And remember, trendy courses such as media studies and communication do not guarantee you a job on a national newspaper or at Sky TV.

_____

Undoubtedly you probably want a good job after graduating and this will have an influence on your choice of institution

_____

As you won't really know how a course will work out until you get there, it is always good to remember that you can usually switch if it comes to that. It's obviously easier to switch to a subject like English (where at least you have the basics) rather than something like maths or engineering, which require more specific A-levels, but the shortage of candidates in some science subjects means universities are often keen to help you do it.

At Scottish universities the first one or two years are designed to be general before specialising for the next two. This is a chance to try out different subjects – but don't experiment too wildly or you end up with a daft pick and mix bag that doesn't lead anywhere.

So does it matter what course you choose? Yes. No matter how little time you intend spending in the library or the lecture room, and all the boasts you hear about dossing around, there is no getting away from academic work at university. If you hate what you're studying, you'll do badly and you won't enjoy the fun bits.

⇨ The above information is reprinted with kind permission from InterStudent. Visit www.interstudent. co.uk for more information.
© InterStudent

Joining clubs and societies

The range of clubs and societies open to university students is endless and, as well as being a great way to meet other students, being part of a club can also equip you with essential marketable skills

The debating society
Michael Parker, a second year History and Politics student at the University of Newcastle, thinks that his role as president of the University's debating society has put him in a great position when it comes to applying for jobs.

'The skills required in public speaking – style, rhetoric, following a line of argument and thinking on your feet – are all things that I feel are transferable to the employment sector, and are highly desirable.

'If you can handle yourself at the head of a table, speaking confidently for seven minutes on the nuclear situation in Korea, then you can probably handle most situations thrown at you by a variety of jobs.'

Cricket and rowing sports clubs
Sarah Berman, a final year Maths student at Oxford University, also thinks that the experience she has gained through taking up active positions in cricket and rowing clubs will help her career prospects.

'Through being on the committee of sports clubs, I have learned to manage people and delegate responsibility. I have also acquired the basics of accountancy through my work as a club treasurer, and gained event management experience whilst helping organise inter-collegiate rowing races.

'I shall leave Oxford with skills that I'll probably be using for the rest of my working life. One of the most important things I've gained is the ability to organise my time effectively, so I am able to do my work and socialise on top of all of these commitments.

'I may have had a hectic four years but I have absolutely no regrets!'

Develop key business-relevant skills
Michael and Sarah are not the only ones who think their involvement with university clubs and societies will help them secure a good job. Emma Fripp, Arcadia Group Resourcing Manager, agrees.

'Students can develop business-relevant skills through clubs and societies. From a retail perspective, leadership and team working are crucial competencies, and these can often be demonstrated by students who have had specific roles within sporting or even social societies.'

Your involvement with clubs or societies can also be the crucial element that makes your CV stand out amongst a pile of similar CVs from graduate applicants.

Offering a bit more looks great on your CV

'I am often faced with several individuals with suitable academic qualifications,' says Jim Alford, who recruits graduates to work in Sefton Council.

> 'Through being on the committee of sports clubs, I have learned to manage people and delegate responsibility'

'I am therefore looking for those candidates who show they can offer that bit more. Involvement in clubs and societies can be used to demonstrate some of the qualities we are looking for.

'These include general skills such as teamwork, project and people management, and the ability to prioritise. Sometimes involvement in voluntary organisations can also lead to specific qualifications that may be relevant to the workplace.'

Keep a record of all your achievements

To make the most of your experiences with clubs and societies, don't forget to keep a record of challenges you have overcome. Read through this before you attend interviews, as employers will often ask you to describe a situation in which you have used a particular skill.

So if you have captained the Ultimate Frisbee team or led the Swing Dance troupe to glory, don't forget to make the most of it in your job applications.

If you can draw upon specific experiences that present practical evidence of your talents, you'll soon have employers asking you to join their club.

Student housing: the basics

Information from need2know

Halls

If you're about to head off to university, you're probably leaving home for the first time. This is a life-changing experience, and most universities like to cushion the blow by offering most first-years a place in university-controlled accommodation, called halls of residence, or 'halls' for short.

Halls are a good option for first-year students because most of them are all-inclusive, which means that you don't have the worry of paying bills for things like electricity and gas, and in some cases, food. It's also a good way to meet friends who you may wish to live with in future term-times.

Consider it a stepping stone between living at home and being out in the big world by yourself.

Most halls have facilities such as telephones, laundering services and sometimes even shops or bars. Your university should have an accommodation office that can give you guidance on which are the best halls for you.

Living out

If you're more the independent type, then living out of halls could be for you.

Unless you have a large income, it's unlikely that you'll be able to afford a place on your own, so ask your university's accommodation office if they have a list of flatshares.

Living out does mean that you'll have to be responsible for paying a share of the bills and making sure the property remains in a good condition. The quality of student accommodation also tends to vary greatly.

Don't agree to live in a dump just because it's cheap. You'll need somewhere nice to study and comfortable so you can rest; if you're dodging rats or falling masonry it's likely you'll be unable to do either. You can find more advice on 'Renting' and 'Housekeeping' on the Need2Know website.

Living at home

Student debt is higher than ever, and if you're looking at a cheap alternative to solve your accommodation problem at university, why not choose to study somewhere closer to where you're from and live at home?

You may be able to come to some sort of arrangement with your parents with regards to paying rent if you're not so keen on taking out a full student loan. Maybe you could look at getting a part-time job while you study. This will help you pay your way at home and also get you out of the house.

One thing about living at home is that you may feel a little 'out of the loop', as people who live in halls together get to know each other quite quickly. Try and join some sort of club or go to as many student events as you can. This way you can have the benefit of student life from the comfort of your own home without having to live in a student 'dive'.

Student mental health

The stress of student life can trigger a range of mental health problems

A Royal College of Psychiatrists report revealed that there has been a progressive increase in the number of students seeking help for mental health problems, and that they're getting more serious. Around one in 12 students requests counselling for a mental health problem during their time at university. Two-thirds of them are women.

What are the main problems that affect students and how can you recognise them?

Depression

Depression is when you feel sad or low for weeks or months, to such an extent that it interferes with your life and studies. The warning signs are loss of interest in life and a feeling you can't enjoy anything, feeling tired, loss of appetite, finding it harder to make decisions, having problems getting to sleep then waking up too early, and loss of interest in sex.

Bipolar disorder

This used to be called manic depression, but is now known as bipolar disorder. About one in ten people with serious depression will have periods of elation and overactivity.

Eating disorders

Anorexia and bulimia are the main eating disorders that affect students, and both are more common in women. Anorexia involves severe, sometimes life-threatening weight loss. Bulimia is more common, and involves bingeing (eating lots of food) then vomiting or purging with laxatives.

People with bulimia are less easy to spot as they may be normal weight. But the illness can lead to tooth decay, dehydration and abnormalities in the chemistry of the blood, leading to faintness and an irregular heartbeat.

Schizophrenia

This affects around one in 100 people and is equally common in men and women, though more men seem to develop schizophrenia when they're young (between the ages of 15 and 25). In women it usually occurs later in life.

The symptoms may include hallucinations (especially hearing voices), paranoid delusions (false beliefs) and difficulty concentrating and getting motivated to do things as simple as washing up or laundry.

Drugs, drink and mental health

If you're feeling low or stressed, you may be tempted to drown your sorrows in alcohol or relax by smoking cannabis. But this won't make you feel better in the longer term, and could make you feel a lot worse.

Around one in ten cannabis users have unpleasant experiences including confusion, hallucinations, anxiety and paranoia. There's also growing evidence that using cannabis over a long period can double your risk of developing a serious mental illness such as schizophrenia.

Ecstasy and amphetamines can also bring on schizophrenia and amphetamines can induce other forms of psychosis. Any underlying mental disorder could be worsened by drug and alcohol use.

Getting help

If you feel persistently unhappy or that you can no longer cope, don't keep it a secret. Telling someone how you feel, whether it's a friend, counsellor or doctor, may bring an immediate sense of relief.

⇨ Initially, it's a good idea to talk to someone you trust, such as a friend, member of your family or college tutor (especially important if your academic performance is being affected by your disorder). Many mild mental health problems can be resolved this way.

⇨ Most universities and colleges have counselling services staffed by qualified professionals, who offer confidential one-to-one counselling. In counselling you can explore the underlying issues of your unhappiness in a safe environment and develop ways to cope.

⇨ Many student unions offer student-led 'pastoral' services. Although the students involved aren't qualified counsellors, you may prefer to talk about problems such as stress and depression with another student who has personal experience of the pressures of student life. These services can be useful in dealing with practical issues such as accommodation and money problems.

⇨ For more serious or persistent mental health symptoms, see your GP. This is the only way to get prescribed treatment or referral to specialist NHS services.

Students who have or develop a mental health condition that requires treatment need to arrange continuity of care between their college doctor and family GP. If moving between university and home results in a gap in treatment, students can make their condition worse.

13 August 2008

⇨ The above information is reprinted with kind permission from NHS Choices. Visit www.nhs.uk for more information.

© NHS Choices

Smoking, alcohol, drugs

Studies show that students are more likely to drink, smoke and take drugs than the general population

Peer pressure, cheap student bars and the freedom of living away from home are big temptations. Be aware of the dangers associated with smoking, drinking and taking drugs so you can make an informed decision about the way you live your life and care for your health.

Alcohol

Student life can seem to revolve around alcohol, with the student bar and local pubs often the centre of the college social scene.

Drinking in moderation is an enjoyable and usually harmless feature of student life. Getting drunk regularly can have potentially serious physical, social and academic effects. Even drinking to excess just occasionally can be damaging.

In the short term, drinking too much can impair academic performance because your concentration will be worse and you're more likely to miss classes, hand in your work late and do badly in exams.

But it can also put you at immediate risk of serious situations ranging from date rape to car crashes. If you're drunk, you're also more likely to be a victim of violence or to have unprotected sex, which carries all the associated risks of sexually transmitted infections (STIs) and unplanned pregnancy.

In the longer term, regularly drinking too much can cause liver disease, an increased risk of heart attack, weight gain and a number of different cancers. Such problems are now occurring at younger ages as alcohol use has increased.

The healthy choice in the short-term is to take just a little extra care to protect yourself and your friends when you are going out drinking (for instance, know your own limits and make sure you know how to get home safely). If you have had a heavy drinking session, you should remain alcohol-free for a full 48 hours to give your body tissues time to recover.

In the longer-term, you do need to have an idea how much you're drinking on a regular basis, in units of alcohol, so you can keep your risks low. The NHS recommends:
⇨ Men should not regularly drink more than three to four units a day.
⇨ Women should not regularly drink more than two to three units a day.

If you're not sure if you're drinking too much go to the DrinkCheck website (www.drinkcheck.nhs.uk).

Student life can seem to revolve around alcohol

Smoking

As with alcohol, there can be a lot of social pressure for students to smoke. Whether you smoke already, or are a non-smoker tempted to take up the habit, consider the risks.

Smoking increases your risk of lung cancer and heart disease. It prematurely ages the skin by up to 20 years and triples your chance of getting wrinkles around your eyes and mouth. It also causes impotence and reduced sperm count in men and reduces fertility in women.

It can lead to gum disease, makes the body store fat around the waist and increases the risk of cellulite.

Don't assume that smoking will help you through the stress of exams. Medical evidence shows that smoking doesn't calm you down. It's simply that nicotine cravings between cigarettes make you feel stressed and anxious so when you have one you feel temporarily calm. You'll feel less stressed once you quit and no longer have cravings.

If you're already a smoker, this could be the ideal time to quit. Going to university or college is a fresh start and a new way of life, and this is your chance to start your new life in a positive, healthy way.

Drugs

Almost half of 16- to 24-year-olds in England and Wales have tried drugs at least once, most commonly cannabis. Experimenting with drugs can sometimes be presented as part of the student experience.

But drugs are illegal for a reason. Aside from the risks to your mental and physical health, using drugs can make you more likely to have unprotected sex, which in turn can increase your risk of being infected with an STI.

A small but significant proportion of regular drug users can come to rely on cannabis or become addicted to drugs such as heroin or cocaine. Any such addiction can have a disastrous effect on your studies and your health.

The legal penalties for drug possession can be severe for some drugs, up to seven years in prison for the possession of a Class A drug like cocaine. Also, your university will not look kindly on you if you're arrested for drug possession. Many universities would ban you from campus, or drop you from your course.

The best way to minimise the risk from drugs is not to use them. Failing that, find out as much information as you can about any drugs you're using, including the risks, the potential for addiction and what happens when you mix one drug with another or with alcohol.

For more information on drugs and their effects, call the confidential FRANK helpline on 0800 776600 or visit the FRANK website (www.talktofrank.com).
13 August 2008

⇨ The above information is re-printed with kind permission from NHS Choices. Visit www.nhs.uk for more information on this and other related topics.

© *NHS Choices*

Student drinking problems

College drinking games can be the start of lifelong addiction

For many new students at UK colleges and universities, freshers' week is a time to have fun, make friends and, in many cases, to drink to excess. In fact, it's safe to say that binge drinking is viewed as 'the norm' at British universities and a large proportion of the undergraduate population appear to be willing participants in the drinking games that are organised as an introduction to college life.

The stakes may be higher than they think. The parents of a Warwick University student, who died in 2006 after drinking half a litre of vodka in 20 minutes for a bet, recently called for urgent action over the 'drinking game' culture in our universities. Back in February, Exeter University announced a ban on all student society initiation ceremonies after a first-year student drank himself to death at the start of the 2006/07 academic year.

It's safe to say that binge drinking is viewed as 'the norm' at British universities

The long-term risks are equally grave, says Sue Allchurch, research director at Linwood Group. 'What many students don't realise is that they may develop bad habits early on that will stay with them for the rest of their student days and into their subsequent careers. This kind of drinking pattern can quickly spiral out of control and lead to alcohol addiction,' she warns. Students should not be fooled into thinking that, as long as they're careful about drinking too much during the week, a 'session' on a Friday or Saturday night does not constitute a problem. In fact, she says, that kind of drinking can carry more risks, because binge

drinkers drink more over a shorter period of time and inflict more long-term physical damage. 'Alcoholism is a progressive illness – over time, the binges will become closer together. If you tell yourself that you are alright because your drinking only goes out of control every few weeks, you are already in denial,' she warns. There are other danger signs, too. These include:

⇨ Blackouts – periods of time you cannot account for when drunk;
⇨ Regularly missing lectures or other commitments due to a hangover or the need to drink instead;
⇨ Daytime drinking in the week – worse still if you do this alone;
⇨ Craving alcohol;
⇨ Drinking in the morning to control a hangover or the shakes;
⇨ Injuring yourself repeatedly when drunk;
⇨ Having attempted to cut back, finding it impossible;
⇨ Making excuses (for example, I only drink lager, I know someone who drinks a lot more than me, all students drink a lot);
⇨ Getting annoyed or defensive if someone mentions the amount you drink.

Student life has much more to offer than hangovers, muddled memories and entirely avoidable accidents and no-one should miss out on the opportunities to grow and learn that are open to them during this important period of their lives. If you, or someone you care about, is struggling with student drinking, confidential help and advice is available from Linwood Group.

30 October 2008

⇨ The above information is reprinted with kind permission from Linwood Group. Visit www.lynwodemanor.co.uk for more information.

© Linwood Group

Student costs breakdown

Will you need more than the change down the back of your sofa? Undoubtedly

The cost of basic student life varies from town to town, and from college to college. Your student union will be able to give you advice specific to your area, and the housing office can give you more information about what to expect to pay in rent.

There are always certain expenses for which you have to plan ahead and budget, so make sure you're aware of the following outgoings...

Rent

The biggie. Student halls might charge an all-in fee that includes rent, electricity, cleaning and food. Increasingly they are becoming self-catering flats where you do your own grub and everything is metered. If you don't have a washing machine, figure in some extra money for launderette prices, and if you're hiring a telly don't forget rental fees and licence money (they will catch up with you sooner or later).

Bills

If you're in a student house, you may have meters for electricity and gas, or quarterly bills. Organise a system so that everyone pays their fair share. The best way to save money is to pay for them online.

Food and other groceries

This should cover everything from cooking at home, to eating out, snacks, coffees, and toiletries and

cleaning products. Sharing things like bread, butter, milk and condiments can help save money.

Tuition fees

If you're unlucky and have to cough up for these, it's a maximum of £3,225 for the academic year 2009/10, usually payable in two or more instalments. More fortunate souls are only forced to pay part of it, or get off the hook completely depending on their parents' income. Contact your LEA (Local Education Authority) to find out where you stand, or check out the Aim Higher website.

Books and equipment

You don't have to buy everything on the reading list, or get the brand new books, but you will need to get a few useful books and whatever else is on your equipment list. Some stuff can be bought cheaper second-hand. Look on your student website to see if any students in the year above are selling the books that you need. Wait until the course has started before buying. That way you can work out what you really need, and use the library as much as possible to keep costs down.

Stationery and photocopying

Computer disks, paper, folders, photocopies of research papers and chapters in books you don't want to buy. It all adds up. Your university department may offer free or subsidised photocopying and equipment, so find out.

Going out

Figure in enough for a social life, and stuff for sports, clubs and other interests. Otherwise, you'll end up bored and lonely, which is not the point of going away to uni.

Travel costs

This covers bus fares, petrol, train tickets, late-night taxis and more. Get hold of discount cards and season passes as early as possible. Book fares in advance to get the best deals.

Clothes

Many stores offer a 10% discount when you can prove you're a student. And remember the golden rule: if you don't ask, you don't get. Not all shops advertise their discounts, but once you flash your student ID their generous sides might get the better of them.

Phone and Internet bills

Keeping in touch can be costly, whether it's paying off your ISP or topping up the credit on your mobile. Shop around for the best deals.

The cost of basic student life varies from town to town, and from college to college

---

Insurance

This is well worth having, especially if it's a student deal. Think about how much it would cost to replace everything you own.

Interest and fines

It is better to take things back to the library, and avoid upsetting the bank manager by going over your overdraft limit unexpectedly, but sometimes it can't be helped. So, if you're absent minded, or cavalier when it comes to cash machine withdrawals, allow a little bit to pay the price for it.

So if you put all those bills together, what do you get? Find out how much money you'll have left at the end of the month with our budget planner.

⇨ The above information is reprinted with kind permission from TheSite. org. Visit www.thesite.org for more information.

© TheSite.org

Push releases figures for 2009 student debt survey

New students should expect to owe £23,500, Push survey reveals

The UK's largest survey of student finance, published today on Push.co.uk, reveals that students who started at university last year can expect to owe nearly £21,200 by the time they leave and new students should reckon on at least £2,000 more than that.

The annual survey by Push, the UK's leading independent resource for prospective students, has found that student debt has topped £5,000 for each year of study for the first time. The inflation-busting increase of 10.6% may in part be down to availability of part-time and temporary jobs during the recession.

The Push Student Debt Survey is the most detailed annual analysis of students' financial position and this year's is the largest to date, involving face-to-face interviews with over 2,000 students at 137 university campuses throughout the UK.

Prospective students receiving their A-level results on Thursday will be particularly concerned as some sources of income have been drying up while debt rises. Other research by Push.co.uk suggests that 80% of students rely on part-time or holiday jobs to supplement their income by an average of £2,000 a year, but these jobs are getting harder to find.

The different funding arrangements around the UK are also reflected in the data. In Scotland, which has the most generous funding system, debts have actually fallen to £2,194 a year and are much lower than the rest of the UK. Meanwhile, with an average of £5,271, students in England owe £205 for each year more than the national average.

The national average projected debt on graduation stands at £15,812, but at six universities, the figure has already broken the £25,000 barrier

---

There is considerable variation between individual universities too. The national average projected debt on graduation stands at £15,812, but at six universities, the figure has already broken the £25,000 barrier. However, at 20 universities, most of which are in Scotland, borrowing is likely to remain under £10,000.

The figures posted today on Push.co.uk form part of the website's detailed profiles of every university in the UK, covering every aspect of student life from teaching standards to the price of beer on each campus.

With university clearing starting on Friday, Push.co.uk features exclusive, insider information on finding the right university and tips to give your application the edge. The website also boasts the 'Uni Chooser' tool, the uniquely powerful search-and-sort facility which enables students to find the university most suited to them.

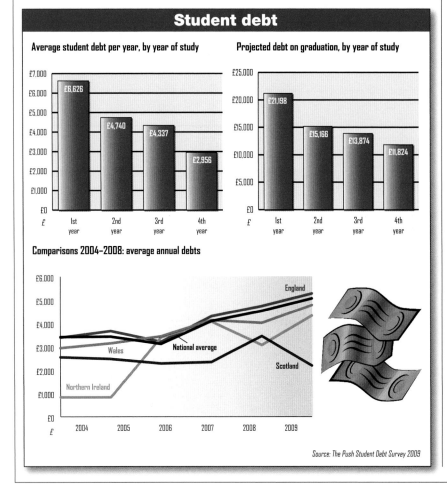

Student debt

Average student debt per year, by year of study

Projected debt on graduation, by year of study

Comparisons 2004-2008: average annual debts

Source: The Push Student Debt Survey 2009

Johnny Rich, Editor of Push.co.uk, commented:

'With the economy in recession, students are even more concerned about debt than they have been in recent years. Finding part-time work has got harder and many students are facing real financial hardship and are worrying about what lies ahead. Even so, the advantages of having a degree still vastly outweigh the costs and the Push survey shows that – with high-quality advice and information – students can keep their debts down while still enjoying the benefits of university.

'These figures beg the question whether we've now passed the point where students can be expected to stump up any more towards their education'

'These figures will give next year's review of student funding a real headache. They beg the question whether we've now passed the point where students can be expected to stump up any more towards their education.'

18 August 2009

⇨ The above information is reprinted with kind permission from Push. Visit www.push.co.uk for more information.

© *Push*

Survey puts spotlight on commercial debt

Commercial debt is by far the biggest fear for students, according to a new survey of more than 6,000 students in Scotland

The survey, *Overstretched and Overdrawn*, conducted by NUS Scotland to look at the impact of the credit crunch on students this summer, also highlights the numbers of students working long hours to try to minimise their overdrafts and credit card debts.

The main findings of the survey include:

⇨ More than half of the students surveyed are in commercial debt, and two-thirds are in debt to friends and family;

⇨ Students from poorer backgrounds are more likely to be concerned about commercial debt, with young students being less afraid of debt than mature students;

⇨ More than half of the students surveyed were in work, with 70 per cent of these working more than the recommended ten hours a week during term-time;

⇨ Students who are in commercial debt are more likely to be in work than other students.

NUS Scotland President, Liam Burns, said 'Our survey has clearly shown that the Government is absolutely right to be concerned about student debt, but the subtlety of what kind of debt will determine whether this Government delivers for students or not. In the reality of the limited amount of support being offered, simply moving from loans to grants is not what is needed. Far worse is the social injustice that would be reinforced if commercial debt is not dealt with, as poorer students are more afraid of commercial debt than those of a luckier background.

'Our response to the Government's consultation on additional student support not only provides grants to the very poorest students and support for student parents, but it starts us on a road to dealing with the reality of the current economic climate for students in alleviating commercial debt, and stopping Scotland's students from becoming even more overdrawn and overstretched.'

Summer 2009

⇨ The above information is reprinted with kind permission from the NUS. Visit www.nus.org.uk for more information.

© *NUS*

Gender and higher education

Extent of under-performance by male students in higher education revealed for the first time in new research from leading higher education think tank

Research to be published today (7 June 2009) by the Higher Education Policy Institute (HEPI) shows the extent of the out-performance of males by females in higher education. The higher education participation rate for women is now 49.2%, whereas it is just 37.8% for men. Women have nearly reached the Government's 50% target while men have a long way to go.

Commenting on the research findings, HEPI's Director, Bahram Bekhradnia, said: 'Some may regard that as an inconvenient fact, and dismiss it by saying that the better performance of women is illusory because, they say, women attend less prestigious institutions, attend part-time rather than full-time, and get less good degrees. Our research shows that all of these assertions are untrue.'

HEPI's research reveals that:
⇨ Women have the same participation as men for Oxford and Cambridge.
⇨ They also have higher participation rates than men for the Russell group and for other old universities, as well as for new universities, for other higher education institutions and for further education colleges too.
⇨ There are more full-time women as well as part-time; and both young and older women have higher participation rates than men.
⇨ There are differences in subject patterns, but in most subjects women outnumber men.
⇨ There are some subjects where men are more numerous – for example in computer science, engineering and the physical sciences – but women outnumber men in popular high status subjects like law and medicine.
⇨ And the relatively poor performance of men occurs throughout society – it's true of middle-class as well as of working-class males, and it occurs in all ethnic groups.
⇨ Once at university, women continue to outperform men. They are more likely to obtain good degrees while men are more likely to drop out. If they do graduate, men are more likely to be unemployed or in non-graduate jobs. However, if they are employed, male graduates are, on average, better paid.

What is astonishing is that this is a phenomenon common to most of the developed world and beyond. The OECD publish data that compare participation rates in higher education: the English (and UK) experience is repeated in almost all other OECD member countries and beyond – it is, for example, a fact in the Arab world no less than it is in the West.

Within England the nature of the GCSE exam and the teaching that is associated with it seem to be part of the reason for the difference in performance at school, and so eventually into and through university, and the report discusses the evidence for this.

Bahram Bekhradnia continues: 'The under-performance of males in HE matters: graduates after all tend to form the elites of society. As women have come to dominate in higher education, we should expect these elites to change gender over time too. That itself is no bad thing. What is intolerable is that significant numbers of young (and not so young) people are excluding themselves – or perhaps being excluded because of aspects of our school system – from joining these elites.'
7 June 2009

⇨ The above information is reprinted with kind permission from the Higher Education Policy Institute (HEPI). Visit www.hepi.ac.uk for more.
© HEPI

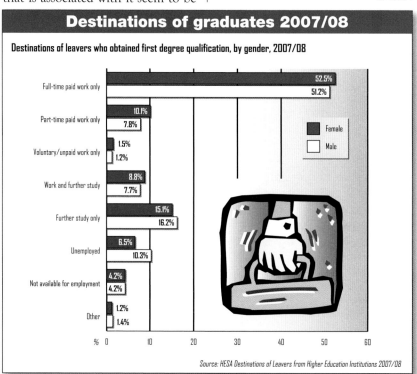

Destinations of graduates 2007/08

Destinations of leavers who obtained first degree qualification, by gender, 2007/08

Destination	Female	Male
Full-time paid work only	52.5%	51.2%
Part-time paid work only	10.1%	7.8%
Voluntary/unpaid work only	1.5%	1.2%
Work and further study	8.8%	7.7%
Further study only	15.1%	16.2%
Unemployed	6.5%	10.3%
Not available for employment	4.2%	4.2%
Other	1.2%	1.4%

Source: HESA Destinations of Leavers from Higher Education Institutions 2007/08

Does a degree really set you up for life?

For generations the prevailing wisdom has been the same: get a good degree and you're set for life. But is that true in 2008? With the recession biting, education debt soaring and the graduate job pool shrinking, are there better ways to get ahead? Here we ask parents, students, graduates and refuseniks if higher education is still the best option

In the haste to bundle one's difficult teenagers off to university, it can easily slip your mind to ask them if they actually want to go. For those of us who have suffered the earache of marching our children at gunpoint through A-levels, this doesn't seem the time to entertain doubts that they might be unsuited to an academic environment. They have to go, and that's it. What else is there?

I used to warn my eldest son – who is still recovering from his freshers' fortnight – that the choice was swotting for exams or wasting his life in a dead-end job. The joke of course is that there aren't enough dead-end jobs to go round. When I left school at 16 in the early seventies, our town offered a variety of unskilled employment – the sauce factory, the dyeworks, the bins – while three O-levels could get you a job as the managing director of the Yorkshire Bank. No one knew anyone with a degree.

We don't have factories now, and Britain has long been banging the drum for the benefits of hard study. Today there are twice as many 25-year-olds with degrees than there were 18-year-olds with A-levels in the sixties. Even I have a degree, having gone back to school in the eighties as a 'mature' student of 27. Higher education took an exciting turn in 1993 when the polys were transformed into universities, gathering speed in 2000 when Tony Blair declared his aim of turning half of all under-30s into graduates by 2010. Would under-

By Phil Hogan, Hermione Hoby, Ally Carnwath, Imogen Carter and Ed Parshotam

achievers from poorer backgrounds be lured by the promise of lifetime earnings at £400,000 above those without degrees? Perhaps 50 per cent seemed possible then, with the figure already at 39.2 per cent, but by last year it had only crept up to 39.8. The ambition remains though. The new higher education minister, David Lammy, says: 'Labour has been working tirelessly to raise aspirations in communities like mine in Tottenham, where not many young people grow up thinking university is for them. Our hard work is paying off – over 50 per cent of young people from every social class say they want to go to university. So our target is a way of showing our determination to make their dreams a reality. The Tories think the trouble with higher education is that too many of other people's kids go to university these days.'

And they do – there are three times more students today (about 2.4m) than in the early eighties, though snipers are quick to point out that many of them are attracted to golf studies and surfing theory. To be fair, in the 19th century they made the same jibes about history, but it is the sort of thing that gets people wondering whether the race to 'widen participation' is such a great idea.

It is vexed at all ends. Students – fearful of piling up debt and ending up with a 'McJob' – complain about poor standards of teaching; tutors complain about poor standards of student literacy, and everybody else complains about the gold standard of A-levels turning into chocolate coins, and that what Britain really needs is more plumbers. Which is true. And not just plumbers. Many talented school leavers are waving goodbye to academia and diving straight into hands-on training or setting up in business, helped by energetic charitable foundations such as Young Enterprise and Edge, whose chairman Gary Hawkes says: 'Our work to combat the perception that vocational and practical learning is a second-class option is crucial to the well-being of our future generations, and to our country's economic vitality.'

For those less bullish about their motor skills and entrepreneurial nous, university is still the place to spend your A-levels – somewhere to turn raw, binge-drinking *joie de vivre* into something noble and fine. Many would add 'marketable' to that, though

I am still glued to the idea of education for the adventure of it, on the grounds that thinking long and hard for three years, even about surfing, might teach you how to think in general. And where better to grow up, smoke, learn to cook and contract an unpleasant disease than 100 miles from home? As Prof Edward Acton, pro-vice-chancellor of the University of East Anglia, says: 'Going to university is the fastest, most agreeable way to gain confidence and enhance one's creativity. A society rich in critically thinking graduates is best equipped to build and sustain the good life.'

Yet all is not well. The drop-out rate is 22 per cent, despite the Government pumping £800m into schemes designed to plug the leak. For these escapees (they are more likely to be at Bolton and Sunderland than Oxford or Cambridge), something has gone wrong. And current job prospects are not great, with traineeships dwindling, recruitment moribund, banking in tatters. Where, you ask, is your £400,000 coming from? Where do you go from here? Back to your parents' house? No one wants that.
PH

Polly Stevenson: the schoolgirl rebel
'I'd rather work and travel'
Sees a degree just for the sake of it as a waste of money, and intends to be surfing in Australia while her peers are swotting.

At her fee-paying school in Essex, 17-year-old Polly Stevenson's attitude to university is not one shared by her peers or teachers. She explains: 'I don't want to go and just do a random degree – I want it to count towards something I want to do when I'm older. It seems a big waste of money if I don't know what I'm going to do with it.' But cost, she's found, isn't something teachers talk about. 'My school's attitude is ridiculous. They're basically like: "Go to university or you don't have a life." Teachers just want us to go because it looks good for the school. I don't think they really care what we do as long as it makes the school look good.'

Out of her year group of more than 100 girls, almost all are going to university, but Polly's bucking the

trend with plans to do a lifeguard qualification and then work for an activity holiday company abroad. 'I've been saving up for years and years, and I've got my heart set on Australia – that's the first place I'm going to go as soon as I've got the money.' She jokes that she'll be a tanned goddess, surfing to work while her friends are stuck here writing essays and getting into debt. Most of them, she complains, 'don't even think about the cost of university; they just have no concept of money because lots of them are quite well off. It's really annoying because I've worked since I was 14 and I'm quite careful with my money.'

41% of current students are given or lent money by friends or family to survive at university

---

Her first job was a paper round. While studying for GCSEs she also took on weekend shifts in a bar and part-time work in a high street shop. With three jobs on the go she admits: 'I pretty much died. My teachers weren't happy about it.' Her parents' attitude was different: 'They were really keen on me getting a job because I have to pay for so many things myself.' Her mother is a social worker and her father is a carpenter: 'They support me as much as they can but my dad wants to retire and hasn't been working as much so we don't have loads of money at the moment.' It's understandable then, that the cost of university strikes her as exorbitant: 'I definitely think university's too expensive – it's thousands and thousands of pounds. I think it's ridiculous that people build up these massive debts and still have them when they're 30.'
HH

Tom Mursell: the refusenik
'A degree is no longer a golden ticket to a good job'
Seeing graduates stacking shelves led Tom to change direction. Now he runs a jobs website called notgoingtouni. co.uk

Like most middle-class teenagers, Tom Mursell, 19, had always assumed he'd go to university after A-levels. He won a place at his first choice, Bournemouth, to study law. 'I had my heart set on that until just before I had to decide whether I was going or not,' he says. 'I really left it right up to the last minute because I wasn't sure.' A moment of realisation in Sainsbury's proved the cataylst for his decision not to go. 'All through college I was working stacking shelves. Then one day I realised that there were graduates doing the same job as me, not using their degree.'

Having decided to take a year out, and resenting 'shocking career advice, almost all of it focused on university', he began to have an idea for a website inspired by his own experiences. From a laptop at his kitchen table in Southampton he started work on notgoingtouni.co.uk as a hobby. Now, with an investor on board and the site set to launch fully in a few months, it's a full-time job. Although Tom's parents – both graduates – were happy about him not going to university, Tom acknowledges that 'a lot of people, especially of my parents' generation, think a degree's a golden ticket to employment. That's not necessarily the case any more though.'

The website is: 'A split between careers adviser and job advertisements – a sort of non-graduate milkround, that's our mission.' Everything suggests that now is a perfect time for such a mission. He plans to become an online entrepreneur, and Channel 4 is following him for a documentary series.

Government targets of 50 per cent of young people in higher education by 2010 are, in his words, 'ridiculous, especially now, with the higher debts and the economic crisis that we're in.

'It's not right to be pushing so many people towards university.'
HH

Jack Forsdike: the disappointed graduate
'All my study is only useful for pub quizzes'
Graduated in film studies from Sheffield Hallam University in May. Now works for a security firm,

providing stewarding at festivals and events.

After three years and thousands of pounds in tuition fees, Jack Forsdike can only think of one area in which he has benefited from his degree. 'All I can use the information for are trivial things,' he says. 'It's the kind of information that comes up in pub quizzes.'

When he left school in 2004 he did not originally plan to go to university. But having been unable to break into a career with the police, he applied through clearing for a place at Sheffield Hallam a year later. He was accepted on a course entitled 'Society in Cities', which he hoped would help him reapply to the police, but soon discovered it was not sociology-based, and switched to film studies.

'It was a topic I felt was going to hold my interest for three years as opposed to something that I wouldn't feel motivated to go to university [each day] and do.'

He enjoyed his studies but as the course progressed began to worry it was not equipping him with skills he'd be able to use after university. 'There was an ongoing catching-up on 100 years of film but it didn't seem applicable in any other area. It started to make me think: how is this going to help set me apart from people who I'm going to be up against when applying for work?'

After graduating, the 22-year-old found employers were unimpressed by his qualification and unconvinced by the skills he had picked up during his degree. 'You're always going to get some people thinking it's a Mickey Mouse degree. But at school [you're told], you get a degree, and no matter what you get it in, it shows an employer you have spent a long time in education.

'It seems like employers don't see it that way. It's either, you've got a degree in the wrong thing or you are lacking experience.'

He now finds himself in exactly the same position he was four years ago, biding his time in temporary work while waiting for South Yorkshire police to recruit again. 'It would have been better if I hadn't gone to university,' he says. 'There's a lot of pressure on people to go who aren't going to benefit from it. I've finished university and I'm seeing friends starting again at the bottom.'
AC

Rising by degrees: paying for university

1962: The Education Act introduces maintenance grants for students on most full-time courses.

1963: Colleges of advanced technology are upgraded to universities.

1979: 679,010 British students attend undergraduate courses.

1990: The Student Loans Company is set up to make up for falling grants.

1992: Polytechnics are granted the right to become universities.

1997: The Dearing Report recommends the end of universal free education and the introduction of student tuition fees. All full-time undergraduates have to contribute £1,000 per year of study on a means-tested basis.

2001: 39% of under-30s are university educated in Britain. At the beginning of the 1980s, 12.5% of schoolchildren went on to university. In his election manifesto Blair announces the Labour Party's aim to raise participation to 50% by 2010.

2006: Following the 2004 Higher Education Act, university top-up fees become law: students must pay up to £3,070 towards each year of a course funded by loans. Scotland had a separate funding system which involved a single £2,000 fee, but this was abolished in April 2008. Wales adopts the same system as England but Welsh students at Welsh universities pay £1,200 a year, means-tested.

2006: 1,636,205 British students take undergraduate courses at British universities.
IC

Uni by numbers: facts and figures

⇨ £3,145 – Maximum annual tuition fee contribution for a British student.

⇨ £9,000 – Median cost of a classroom-based undergraduate degree per annum for international students.

⇨ £10,700 – Median cost of a laboratory or workshop-based undergraduate degree per annum for international students.

⇨ 54% of current students are concerned about debt.

⇨ 41% of current students are given or lent money by friends or family to survive at university. Of them, 26% get regular amounts throughout the term.

⇨ £19,000 – Median starting salary for a new graduate in full-time employment.

⇨ £21,500 – Projected debt for students starting a degree in 2008.

Does a university degree really help graduates get to the top?

⇨ £14,044 – The average debt that students at the Central School of Speech and Drama in London accrue each year, the highest for any higher education institute in Britain.

⇨ £1,184 – The average debt that students at Robert Gordon University in Aberdeen accrue each year, the lowest for any higher education institute.

⇨ 35% of students hold a term-time job. 51% of students work during the holidays.

⇨ 109 – Universities in the UK.

⇨ 0.8% – The UK's public expenditure on higher education as a percentage of GDP. At 1.8%, Denmark spends the most.

⇨ 80% of UK applicants successfully gained university places through UCAS in 2007.

⇨ 46% – Increase in students studying undergraduate degrees in the UK since 1994–95.

⇨ 113,685 full-time academic staff at UK higher education institutes.

⇨ 37% are female.
EP & IC
9 November 2008 (extract)
© Guardian Newspapers Limited 2010

Boosting social mobility

New million+ report confirms that modern universities boost social mobility

University think-tank million+ today (Monday) published a report which examined the levels of social mobility generated by modern universities.

The report, *Social Mobility: universities changing lives*, defined social mobility in two ways – first as movement into higher status occupations and second, as the opportunity for increased earnings.

Graduates from modern universities earn significantly more than they would had they not gone to university at all

The research analysed data from the Higher Education Statistics Agency (HESA) and found that modern universities are creating significant social mobility by occupation group and showed that graduates from modern universities earn significantly more than they would had they not gone to university at all. The research team interviewed graduates whose lives and prospects had been changed by studying at university and a number of graduate case-studies are included in the report.

Key findings

⇨ On entry to university, 8% of the student cohort came from professional families. Three-and-a-half years after graduating, 17% of these students had similar professional or managerial careers.

⇨ Three-and-a-half years after graduating, wages of graduates from million+ member universities are likely to be nearly 15% higher than wages of people who have lower qualifications, many of whom could have progressed to university but did not do so.

million +

leading the university agenda

⇨ Modern universities have a more diverse student profile, including a higher proportion of black, Asian, female and older students, compared to the average for all UK universities. This provides opportunities for social mobility across a very broad section of the population and in respect of other equality indicators.

⇨ These universities are offering this social mobility on a significant scale and educate over half of the UK's higher education students.

The report argues for a broader perspective to be brought to the policy debate about the social mobility created by universities – rather than one focused on encouraging a few thousand high achievers from working class backgrounds accessing a small number of traditional universities. The report makes the case for generating social mobility through transforming the lives of large numbers of students who otherwise would not have gone to university.

Professor Les Ebdon CBE, Chair of university think-tank million+ and Vice-Chancellor of the University of Bedfordshire, said: 'This report proves the social mobility pessimists wrong. New generations of students have been encouraged by the Government to apply to university. By supporting their aspirations, modern universities have contributed to significant improvements in social mobility.

'We welcome the fact that all of the main political parties in the UK now say they are committed to improving social mobility. They must now be willing to fund universities so that they can meet the demand for university places of students in 2009 and beyond.'

Social Mobility: universities changing lives makes some key recommendations to policymakers and calls for more people to get the chance to progress by going to university. This will require renewed and sustained efforts to widen participation and enhanced investment by Government in university student numbers.

30 March 2009

⇨ The above information is reprinted with kind permission from million+. Visit www.millionplus.ac.uk for more information.

© *million+*

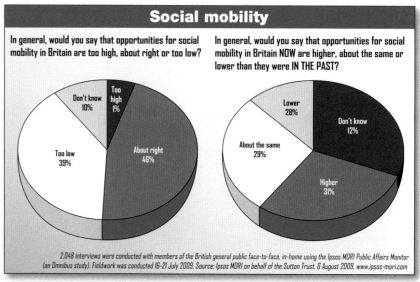

Social mobility

In general, would you say that opportunities for social mobility in Britain are too high, about right or too low?

- Too high 1%
- About right 46%
- Too low 39%
- Don't know 10%

In general, would you say that opportunities for social mobility in Britain NOW are higher, about the same or lower than they were IN THE PAST?

- Lower 28%
- Don't know 12%
- About the same 29%
- Higher 31%

2,048 interviews were conducted with members of the British general public face-to-face, in-home using the Ipsos MORI Public Affairs Monitor (an Omnibus study). Fieldwork was conducted 16-21 July 2009. Source: Ipsos MORI on behalf of the Sutton Trust, 6 August 2009. www.ipsos-mori.com

State school pupils shun top degree courses

Thousands of state school pupils are not applying to the most selective university degree courses despite having the A-levels to secure a place, new research shows

The report reveals that pupils from top-performing independent schools on average make twice as many applications to leading research universities than their peers from state comprehensive schools with similar average A-level results. Application rates from further education colleges, meanwhile, were less than half of those from other types of schools with similar average exam results.

The study also shows that if university participation patterns were the same for those in the state sector[1] in England as independent school pupils with similar 'academic' A-level results, over 4,500[2] extra state school students each year could enter the 500 university courses with the most demanding entry qualifications.

The research, undertaken jointly by the Sutton Trust and the Department for Business, Innovation and Skills, analyses information on hundreds of thousands of students using UCAS applications data and the National Pupil Database.

Chairman of the Sutton Trust Sir Peter Lampl said: 'This research shows that even with the right grades in the right A-level subjects, thousands of state schools each year do not apply to the most academically selective degree courses. Many highly

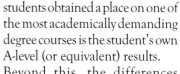

able pupils from non-privileged backgrounds wrongly perceive the most prestigious universities as "not for the likes of us", and often lack the support and guidance to overcome this misconception.

'As well as underlining the continued need for outreach activities like summer schools, with A-level results being published next week, this timely research provides yet another compelling reason to reform the university application system. Students should be able to apply to higher education on the basis of their actual results rather than predicted grades, which can be inaccurate. This simple step towards post-qualification applications would give many non-privileged students the confidence to aim that little bit higher.'

Key findings of the research include:

Overall trends
⇨ The single most important factor determining the probability that

students obtained a place on one of the most academically demanding degree courses is the student's own A-level (or equivalent) results.
⇨ Beyond this, the differences by type of school or college in participation rates on the most academically demanding courses can be largely explained by differences in the number and patterns of applications from different types of school or college.

'Many highly able pupils from non-privileged backgrounds wrongly perceive prestigious universities as "not for the likes of us"'

Application rates
⇨ Pupils from independent schools in the top fifth of schools according to their overall A-level attainment, on average made twice as many applications to 'Sutton 13' universities[3] than their peers from comprehensive schools with similar overall levels of attainment.
⇨ Application rates from FE colleges to 'Sutton 13' universities were less than half of those from other types of schools, even when differences in average overall levels of A-level attainment are taken into account.

Participation rates
⇨ A student with the equivalent of ABB at A-level (including at least one 'core academic' A-level[4]) who attended an independent school has a 79% chance of entering one of the 500 most selective degree

courses, compared with 70% for a similar student attending a state-maintained school.

⇨ If pupils in the state sector in England had the same participation rates as pupils from independent schools with similar 'academic' A-level results, over 4,500 extra students could enter the 500 courses with the highest average entry qualifications by age 19.

⇨ If FE sector students had the same participation rates as those in selective state schools with similar 'academic' A-level attainment, then over 1,000 extra students from the FE sector (including FE and sixth-form colleges) could enter the 500 courses with the highest average entry qualifications by age 19.

Offer rates[5]

⇨ It appears that young people from schools and colleges with similar overall attainment levels and who applied to the most academically demanding universities were about as likely to get an offer whatever the type of school or college they attended.

⇨ Saying this, about a third of applications to 'Sutton 13' universities from those in the lowest-attaining comprehensive schools resulted in offers, but only a fifth of those from FE colleges with similar overall levels of attainment did so.

Notes

1 Including maintained schools, sixth-form colleges and genera/tertiary FE colleges.

2 Made up of 2,333 students from comprehensive schools; 1,277 from FE colleges; 693 from sixth-form colleges; and 315 from selective state schools.

3 These are 13 highly selective universities which came top of an average ranking of the newspaper league tables in 2000: Birmingham, Bristol, Cambridge, Durham, Edinburgh, Imperial College, London School of Economics, Nottingham, Oxford, St Andrews, University College London, Warwick and York.

4 For this analysis, core academic subjects were defined as A-levels in Maths, English, Physics, Chemistry, Biology or History.

5 These findings need to be treated with some caution as they may still reflect differences in individual students' levels of achievement.

July 2009

⇨ The above information is reprinted with kind permission from the Sutton Trust. Visit www.suttontrust.com for more information.

© *Sutton Trust*

New universities to revert to old polytechnic role

By Jack Grimston

The former polytechnics are to take back much of their previous role of providing adult education and vocational degrees rather than trying to ape leading academic institutions under reforms being drawn up by John Denham, the universities secretary.

The change will mark a shift in policy for the Government, which for years has tried to promote the research credentials of 'new' universities alongside those of traditional institutions.

Denham wants top universities like Cambridge to become part of an 'elite'

It follows the eruption of 'class war' between vice-chancellors this year over how to share £1.5 billion of research funding. Universities created since 1992 claim they are entitled to a far higher share than in the past.

> **'The truth is that a classics degree at a traditional university is not the same as a degree in mining and engineering at another'**

In an interview with *The Sunday Times*, Denham also signalled an easing of Labour attacks on Oxbridge 'elitism' long pursued by ministers including Gordon Brown.

Denham instead wants to encourage the emergence of an elite including Oxford, Cambridge and a handful of others. These would receive most research funding, although 'pockets of excellence' in the post-1992 group would also get a fair share.

Denham will launch a strategy for higher education this summer and will give indications of its direction in a speech this week.

The concrete changes will include a fresh form of vocational degree. This will be offered mainly by new universities and will benefit teenagers who take specified vocational qualifications rather than A-levels.

For example, those serving apprenticeships in hotels and restaurants could earn degrees in hotel management, while those with vocational qualifications in building could study part-time for a degree in construction while working on site.

'I want to nurture the different parts of the system,' said Denham. '[For example] research-intensive universities and the ones who do most for part-time and adult education.'

He added: 'The truth is that a classics degree at a traditional university is not the same as a degree in mining and engineering at another.'

Denham has told friends that a country this size can probably support no more than five to ten universities as an equivalent to America's Ivy League.

His remarks will come as a relief to leading universities. Labour has been putting them under relentless pressure to increase the proportion of students they admit from poorer backgrounds.

Denham, who attended a comprehensive in Lyme Regis, Dorset, and Southampton University, acknowledged that post-1992 institutions must take the lead in bringing more working-class pupils into higher education.

'Institutions that take most of the students who would not traditionally have gone to university are in a different position from those that are most research-intensive and selective,' he said. 'We are not expecting those places to be the major places for widening participation.'

He added: 'We can't expect universities to put right the whole welter of social disadvantage, low aspirations, lack of tradition of going to higher education.'

The minister does, however, believe leading universities should put strenuous efforts into encouraging more applications from the 10,000 or so highly able teenagers from poorer families who never even apply, 'perhaps because nobody inspired them'.

Denham's approach is likely to anger vice-chancellors of former polytechnics and dozens of other institutions that have been turned into universities in the past 16 years.

Last week Malcolm McVicar, vice-chancellor of the University of Central Lancashire, warned that dividing institutions by role was 'outdated' and could 'lead to a row that will make the 2005 fees row look like a Sunday afternoon tea party'.

Expanding knowledge

⇨ 1450: There were three universities in Britain – Oxford, Cambridge and St Andrews.

⇨ 1900: Victorian foundations took total to 14.

⇨ 1970: Number more than trebled to 48 with 'red bricks' and 1960s 'plate glass' campuses.

⇨ 1992: Polytechnics became universities, taking total to 86. Typical is the University of Central Lancashire, founded in 1828 as the Preston Institution for the Diffusion of Useful Knowledge.

⇨ There are now 169 higher education institutions, of which 109 are universities.

22 February 2009

© *The Times 2010*

Higher education and earning power

State school pupils fail to recognise differences in universities' earning powers

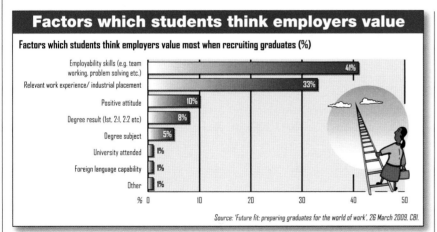

Factors which students think employers value

Factors which students think employers value most when recruiting graduates (%)

Factor	%
Employability skills (e.g. team working, problem solving etc.)	41%
Relevant work experience/ industrial placement	33%
Positive attitude	10%
Degree result (1st, 2:1, 2:2 etc)	8%
Degree subject	5%
University attended	1%
Foreign language capability	1%
Other	1%

Source: 'Future fit: preparing graduates for the world of work', 26 March 2009, CBI.

Half of state school pupils do not think that they will be better off financially by going to certain universities over others, and teachers in the maintained sector are reluctant to discuss the different status of universities, suggest two new pieces of research commissioned by the Sutton Trust.

A survey of over 3,000 young people by PeopleSurv revealed that 51% of those educated in state schools believed there is no difference in earnings between higher education institutions, compared with 35% from independent schools. Young people from poorer backgrounds were also less likely to recognise differences than their better off peers (68% versus 38%), even though studies show that graduates from universities with higher academic status have significantly higher earnings than those from other universities (see note).

In separate research undertaken by the Institute of Education, researchers found that, even in schools with good track records in admissions to highly-selective universities, the emphasis in briefing sessions was on entry to higher education in general: 'Teachers are generally reluctant to draw attention to status differences between universities, and many students appear to have only a vague notion of status.' The exception to this is Oxford and Cambridge, partly because Oxbridge applicants are openly given extra assistance with applications and preparation for interview.

The Institute of Education study also reported that the children with two graduate parents were much more likely than others to discuss university entry at home and were therefore less reliant on information provided by the school. They also began to think about applying to university much earlier in their school careers.

Sir Peter Lampl, Chairman of the Sutton Trust, said: 'The UK's diverse higher education sector has institutions of many different strengths, and it is right that young people consider a range of factors when making their choices.

51% of those educated in state schools believed there is no difference in earnings between higher education institutions, compared with 35% from independent schools

---

'But we believe it is important that all young people should be aware of all the relevant information on different courses at different universities. Pupils should not be disadvantaged in making these decisions by their background or the type of school they happen to attend. We need to spread best practice on information, advice and guidance on higher education choices from a handful of schools and colleges to the rest of the sector.'

The Institute's research built on an earlier Sutton Trust report, which showed that there are relatively few comprehensive schools that send significant numbers of students to the most prestigious universities, and those that do so tend to have relatively advantaged students. The new study sought to identify what factors had enabled a few state comprehensives to have relatively high levels of admission to prestigious universities at the same time as having a higher than average proportion of disadvantaged pupils.

Professor Geoff Whitty, a member of the Institute team, said: 'Even with similar predicted grades, students from families where neither parent went to university are much less likely to apply to prestigious universities than those with two graduate parents. All students, but first-generation students in particular, need earlier information and help from the school if they are to make appropriate choices about which subjects to study and which universities to apply to.

Note

Two forthcoming studies support this:

Wage Returns to Quality of Higher Education Institute Attended *by Iftikhar Hussain, Sandra McNally, Shqiponja Telhaj, London School of Economics*

This study uses data from a series of Graduate Cohort Studies to assess the wages of graduates four years after leaving university. It uses a range of factors – including research ratings in the Research Assessment Exercise, the retention rate for students, average pre-university test scores in A-levels and other exams – to estimate the status of different universities. The calculations control for range of individual characteristics of students including A-level points score, subject of degree, gender, age, type of school attended, ethnicity and parental education. It concludes that the wage returns for graduates from a top-ranked institution using these measures are over twice as high as the returns for graduates from an institution ranked much more lowly. The study also suggests that these differences in returns may be increasing over time.

Graduating and gradations within the middle class: the legacy of an elite higher education *by Sally Power, Cardiff University, and Geoff Whitty, Institute of Education*

This study surveys the outcomes of a small cohort of graduates who left university in the mid-1990s. It creates a ranking of elite universities from various published 'performance' tables. These include Bristol, Cambridge, Durham, Edinburgh, Imperial, King's College London, London School of Economics, Oxford, St Andrews, University College London. It finds that nearly one-fifth (19%) of those who went to elite universities were earning over £90,000 per annum, compared with only 8% and 5% of those who went to other 'old' and 'new' universities, respectively. 33% of the graduates from elite universities now own their home outright, compared with 21% of graduates from other universities and 13% of non-graduates.

21 May 2008

⇨ The above information is reprinted with kind permission from the Sutton Trust. Visit www.suttontrust.com for more information.

© *Sutton Trust*

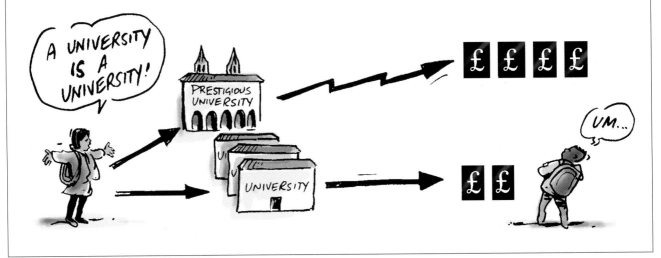

Oxbridge introduce new entrance tests

Students are facing a battery of new tests to get into Oxford and Cambridge amid continuing fears that A-levels fail to mark out the best candidates

**By Graeme Paton,
Education Editor**

More than 70 per cent of Oxford applicants are required to sit a pre-interview entrance exam in subjects such as history, English, languages, mathematics and science this term, compared with 50 per cent just two years ago.

The development has fuelled a dramatic rise in demand for private tutors set up to help teenagers negotiate the admissions process. One company reported a doubling in the number of enquiries for coaching specifically to pass Oxbridge entrance tests.

It comes as record numbers of school-leavers attempt to get into the two universities in 2010. Oxford has already announced a 12 per cent rise in applications.

An increase in entrance tests – sat by thousands of candidates this month – will fuel fears that tutors are finding it increasingly difficult to select the best candidates from record numbers of pupils leaving school with at least three As at A-level.

In the mid-1980s, fewer than half of Oxbridge applicants gained straight As, but this year every candidate is expected to achieve the feat.

Earlier this month, the Government announced a major review of university admissions, suggesting that A-levels should not dictate entry to the most sought-after courses.

Mike Nicholson, Oxford's director of admissions, said: 'Without aptitude tests as part of the admissions process, it would be impossible for Oxford to effectively shortlist candidates for interview in the subjects that are most over-subscribed.

'When we are presented with 17,000 candidates for around 3,200 places, all of whom have glowing references and excellent academic records, aptitude tests and interviews allow us to differentiate between the very best and the very good.'

Applications to Oxford and Cambridge close in October – before the deadline for other universities.

Both institutions largely abolished entrance exams in most subjects in the mid-90s under pressure from state schools, which claimed they discriminated in favour of pupils from the private sector.

But different tests have been slowly reintroduced over the last decade. Oxford insisted they bore almost no resemblance to the old entrance exams.

Students applying for 36 different subjects at Oxford are now required to take a pre-interview aptitude test. Subjects such as experimental psychology and PPP (philosophy, psychology and physiology) were added for the first time this year.

At Cambridge, students take a generic 'thinking skills' tests after applying to study computer science, economics, engineering, land economy, natural sciences and PPS (politics, psychology and sociology) at some colleges. For the first time this year, Cambridge is also running its own law exam after dropping the Law National Admissions Test, which is used to dictate entry to many courses across the country.

Most exams are taken in the first week of November or early December.

Sucedo, a company offering exam coaching, said it had seen a 'massive upsurge' in demand for help to pass admissions tests, particularly from state school students.

A spokesman said: 'Entrance examinations are growing exponentially year-by-year, and will expand beyond Oxbridge soon, in force.'

James Uffindell, founder of Oxbridge Applications, which advises students applying to leading universities, said seminars focusing on entrance exams were over-subscribed this year and sales of mock tests doubled.

15 November 2009

Teachers show alarming Oxbridge misconceptions

Information from the Sutton Trust

Secondary school teachers in England and Wales seriously underestimate the proportion of state school students at Oxford and Cambridge universities, according to an Ipsos MORI survey of nearly 500 teachers published by the Sutton Trust today.

Secondary school teachers in England and Wales seriously underestimate the proportion of state school students at Oxford and Cambridge universities

---

More than a third of those who made a valid response believed that 20% or less of undergraduates at the two universities came from the state sector, and the majority (three-fifths) thought it was 30% or less, even though 93% of school-aged children attend state schools. In total 91% of teachers underestimated the representation of state school pupils, while only 1.5% over-estimated (see graphs below).

Only 8% of respondents picked the correct figure of between 51% and 60% of students coming from the state sector. The actual figure is 54%.

The majority of teachers answering (56%) also thought it was more expensive for students to study at Oxbridge, whereas in fact the two universities charge the same tuition fees as the vast majority of other English universities and offer some of the most generous bursary provision.

Alarmingly, only just over half the teachers (54%) reported that they would generally recommend their brightest students to apply to Oxbridge, while 45% said they would never or rarely do so.

Sir Peter Lampl, Chairman of the Sutton Trust, said: 'The misconceptions among secondary school teachers about Oxbridge are alarming and clearly have an impact on the number of bright state school students applying to these two great universities, despite the considerable efforts that both are making to reach out to them.'

The Sutton Trust sponsors summer schools and other access initiatives at both universities for state school students and teachers. But Sir Peter added: 'It is clear that much more needs to be done to dispel the myths about Oxbridge and other leading universities, and to ensure that young people's higher education decisions are based on fact not fiction.'
11 January 2008

⇨ The above information is reprinted with kind permission from the Sutton Trust. Visit www.suttontrust.com for more information.

© Sutton Trust

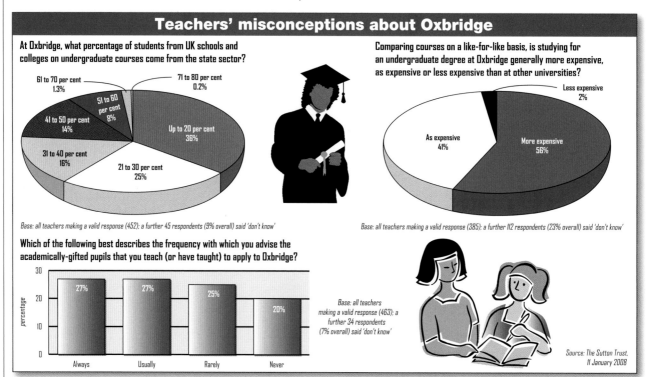

Teachers' misconceptions about Oxbridge

At Oxbridge, what percentage of students from UK schools and colleges on undergraduate courses come from the state sector?

- 71 to 80 per cent 0.2%
- 61 to 70 per cent 1.3%
- 51 to 60 per cent 8%
- 41 to 50 per cent 14%
- 31 to 40 per cent 16%
- 21 to 30 per cent 25%
- Up to 20 per cent 36%

Base: all teachers making a valid response (452); a further 45 respondents (9% overall) said 'don't know'

Comparing courses on a like-for-like basis, is studying for an undergraduate degree at Oxbridge generally more expensive, as expensive or less expensive than at other universities?

- Less expensive 2%
- As expensive 41%
- More expensive 56%

Base: all teachers making a valid response (385); a further 112 respondents (23% overall) said 'don't know'

Which of the following best describes the frequency with which you advise the academically-gifted pupils that you teach (or have taught) to apply to Oxbridge?

Always	Usually	Rarely	Never
27%	27%	25%	20%

percentage

Base: all teachers making a valid response (463); a further 34 respondents (7% overall) said 'don't know'

Source: The Sutton Trust, 11 January 2008

Mandelson outlines the future of higher education

The Government has unveiled a new framework for the future success of higher education, setting out the important role universities will play in securing the country's economic recovery and long-term prosperity

Lord Mandelson's vision to sustain university success in more challenging and competitive times sets out the Government's approach on the major issues facing universities, including the need to make greater contributions to the economy, widening access and strengthening our research capacity.

The higher education framework, Higher Ambitions, sets out a strategy for universities to remain world class, providing the nation with the high-level skills needed to remain competitive, while continuing to attract the brightest students and researchers.

Key measures set out in the framework include:

⇨ More competition between universities, giving greater priority to programmes that meet the need for high-level skills;

⇨ Business to be more engaged in the funding and design of programmes, sponsorship of students, and work placements;

⇨ Creating more part-time, work-based and foundation degrees to make it easier for adults to go to university, with routes from apprenticeships through to foundation degrees and other vocational programmes;

⇨ Encouraging universities to consider contextual data in admissions, as one way of ensuring that higher education is available to all young people who have the ability to benefit;

⇨ Universities setting out clearly what students can expect in terms of the nature and quality of courses offered;

⇨ Sustaining our world-class research base by continuing to focus on excellence, concentrating research funding where needed to secure critical mass and impact; and

⇨ Encouraging collaboration between universities on world-class research, especially in high-cost science.

In the House of Lords, Lord Mandelson said:

'Able people and bright ideas are the foundation stones of a thriving knowledge economy and in the next ten years we will want more, not fewer people in higher education, and more not less quality research.

'We have made great progress in the number of young people going to university at 18 or 19 to do a three-year degree. But the challenge for the next decade is to offer a wider range of new study opportunities – part-time, work-based, foundation degrees and studying whilst at home – to a greater range of people.

'All students must continue to enter higher education on their merit. But I believe this means taking account of a student's academic attainment, their aptitude and their potential. Many universities are already developing their use of contextual data in admissions and we hope that all universities will look at their examples and consider incorporating such data in their admissions processes.

'The Government also want universities to make an even bigger contribution to Britain's economic recovery and future growth.

'We have therefore decided to give greater priority to programmes that meet the need for high-level skills, especially in key areas such as science, technology, engineering and maths. There will be a greater element of competition between universities for new contestable funding as an incentive to fulfil this priority. With employers and universities, we will identify where the supply of graduates is not meeting demand for key skills. And we will seek to re-balance this, by asking HEFCE to prioritise the courses and subjects which match these skills needs.

'We will look to business to be more active partners with our universities. We want employers to be fully engaged in the funding and design of university programmes, the sponsorship of students, and offering work placements.

'In the decade ahead we will expect more from our universities than ever before. They will need to use their resources more effectively, reach out to a wider range of potential students and devise new sources of income, at the same time as they maintain teaching and research excellence.'

The Department for Business, Innovation and Skills also announced that Sir Martin Harris, the Director for Fair Access, will consult with vice chancellors and provide the Government with a report on what further action could be taken to widen access to highly selective universities for those from under-privileged backgrounds.

Lord Mandelson added:

'Wider and fairer access to university is a question of basic social justice and it is right that able students with the talent and ability to attend a highly selective university are given a fair chance to do so, regardless of where they live or the school they attend.'

3 November 2009

⇨ The above information is reprinted with kind permission from the Department for Business, Innovation and Skills. Visit www.bis.gov.uk for more information.

© Crown copyright

How do we tell the good universities from the bad?

By Gaby Hinsliff

One is the oldest university in the English-speaking world, synonymous with dreaming spires and David Cameron's formative years. The other is a former polytechnic whose famous alumni include Panther from the TV series *Gladiators*.

But when the vice-chancellors of Oxford University and its neighbour Oxford Brookes University testified together before a Commons committee last March, they were united on one thing. Asked how a 2:1 in history from one could possibly be worth the same as a 2:1 from the other, given their differing intakes and teaching methods, both went to great lengths to avoid answering.

> If 'different levels of effort are required in different universities' to obtain the same classification, how can we be sure it is not sometimes too easy to get a First?

The exchange became so heated that Phil Willis, chairman of the select committee on innovation, universities and skills, later wrote and apologised. But Oxford University was still smarting this weekend at what a spokesman called the 'inappropriate' demand to compare 'apples and oranges'.

Yet the clash reveals the gulf between the two cultures. For academics, the question was ridiculous: universities differ so widely in syllabuses, teaching methods and expectations of their students they cannot realistically be compared.

But for the politicians, that was precisely the point: they argue that employers and students must be able

to compare degrees, or how can they tell which are worth having? If, as the committee's report today concludes, 'different levels of effort are required in different universities' to obtain the same classification, how can we be sure it is not sometimes too easy to get a First?

'Of course, at the University of Salford, say, there will be a number of exceptional students worthy of the very highest academic achievement,' says Willis. 'But let's not pretend they are going to emerge in the same numbers in Salford as they might at Imperial or UCL.'

But to vice-chancellors, his recommendations – tougher inspection, universal standard for degrees, national bursary system and central code of admissions like that for schools – represents a direct attack on their jealously guarded independence. Universities' ability to decide for themselves who to admit, what to teach and how to award degrees is, they argue, inextricably linked to what Diana Warwick, chief executive of Universities UK, calls the 'spirit of free inquiry', essential to scholarship and creativity. 'If you simply revert to a national curriculum with a national inspectorate, I think that would be a great loss to the UK,' she says.

The Government has so far ducked the row: the new higher education secretary Lord Mandelson insists today that he does not 'recognise the committee's description' of universities.

But his speech last week warning that universities should provide more options for part-time or mature students and for local study near home were seen privately by vice-chancellors as a sign that future Government funding will have more strings attached. And an incoming Tory Government may be even tougher. David Willetts, the Conservative higher education spokesman, says perpetuating myths that all universities are equal is cheating students unfamiliar with the secret pecking order.

'There is a conspiracy in which the Government has been complicit in pretending that universities are all the same,' he says. 'Middle-class parents know that they are not, but if you talk to teenagers at a school that doesn't necessarily send lots of children to university, they don't know that.'

Better information about the real returns on a degree from specific institutions is, he argues, crucial. For what has really galvanised this argument is raw economics. Despite the introduction of variable tuition fees, there is no real market in higher education: students almost without

exception pay £3,225 in tuition fees to study, wherever they go.

But this autumn, ministers will review the case for a rise and for more variation, encouraging colleges to charge more for popular courses and less for under-subscribed subjects. Students asked to pay up to £7,000 will question whether some institutions are worth it – and that could drive weaker colleges to the brink.

Gillian Evans is an internationally renowned lecturer in ecumenical theology. And if you are not entirely familiar with that branch of mediaeval history, you are not alone.

'There are probably six people in the world who really know what I do,' says Evans, an Oxford don and expert in university regulation. 'And the last thing they want to do is waste their own precious time evaluating it.'

Which means universities cannot be treated like schools, she argues, because evaluating the marking of a dissertation on cutting-edge astrophysics or an esoteric branch of philosophical thought requires a much rarer level of expertise than ticking a teenage maths test. Besides, even if all courses taught the same curriculum, the cachet of some colleges would persist: 'There is no way that coming out with an Oxford or Cambridge degree isn't for the foreseeable future going to be an advantage.'

Willis, however, argues that it must be possible at least to examine 'academic rigour' in different universities – and that the system is failing to do so now.

At present, university exams are marked internally and that marking is then assessed by external examiners, with the process overseen by the Quality Assurance Agency on behalf of the Higher Education Finance Council for England, which distributes university funding in England and Wales.

However, the committee concluded that the QAA was not actually measuring academic standards, merely supervising a process, and had few powers to intervene when standards slipped: it recommends radically changing its remit and, if that does not work, scrapping it.

Where both sides agree is that there is too little academic research to explain why 61% of students now get a First or 2:1, compared to 53% in 1997. Are students getting brighter, standards lower, or lecturers better? What impact did the rising number of girls, who have consistently outperformed boys in school exams, going to university have?

Are degrees from different universities all worth the same?

One study examined by the committee, from Professor Mantz Yorke at Lancaster University, cited factors including better teaching and more diligent students but also the significance for universities of doing well in league tables.

Evans also blames league tables but cautions that this is, by academic standards, just a hunch: 'We don't actually know if there is a problem until the research has been done into what happened as a consequence of the post-1992 changes [when polytechnics became universities].'

The phenomenon is certainly not unique to Britain – in the US, concern over steadily rising grade point averages has even prompted Princeton to cap the percentage of students who could get As – but shot up the British agenda last year after academic whistleblowers complained of pressure to boost the grades of undeserving candidates. A leaked email sent to maths faculty staff at Manchester Metropolitan University asked them to bear in mind an 'understandable desire to increase'

the number of Firsts and 2:1s it awarded when marking.

A senior lecturer at the university, Walter Cairns, told the committee he had failed 85% of students on one law course, only to have the marks pushed up without his consent. He was kicked off the university's governing board after testifying and only reinstated after the committee complained, an attitude to whistleblowers that Willis argues remains too prevalent.

'There is a conspiracy in which the Government has been complicit in pretending that universities are all the same'

Other witnesses complained of pressure to provide higher grades after marking down work that was, as one put it, 'almost impossible to follow, largely empty of content, a regurgitation of lecture notes or basic textbooks, and factually incorrect'. The report also found British students had less 'face time' with tutors than abroad and appear to work less hard, putting in 30 hours of study a week while US students did twice that.

Where both the committee and universities agree is that tackling quality is critical to the drive for more students to study closer to home – a cheaper option in a world where higher education is likely to become more expensive.

Unless middle-class parents can be convinced their local university is as good as the best, that is likely to fail.

When a handful of universities last week declined to participate in the Government's plan for 10,000 extra student places this year to meet that demand, arguing that the extra places were underfunded and had too many strings attached, it was a small but significant show of defiance. Easing recession may be the Government's priority but it was not, the revolt suggested, top priority for centres of academic excellence.

Nonetheless, Universities UK is lobbying hard against funding cuts, on the grounds that to starve universities would slow down the economic recovery.

'If there are going to be cuts in public expenditure, higher education may be asked to take its share,' says Warwick. 'That is bound to have an impact on the number of students they can take: I think Government will recognise that is not a sensible thing to do at a time when what we need to do is provide higher numbers of skills for larger numbers of people.'

Nonetheless, redundancies have already begun at some universities. Even before the recession, UK universities were under pressure from overseas competition – particularly China and India. And that threatens one of its most lucrative sources of income, foreign students. Vice-chancellors are privately debating closer ties to the private sector to plug anticipated gaps in state funding.

And it is clear that under a Tory Government, universities may find themselves vying for students with more private and not-for-profit rivals setting up in Britain too. 'There are American university chains that are looking to come into Britain, talk of mergers between British and American universities. India is looking at links. I think it's ripe for these kind of supply-side reforms,' says Willetts.

Warwick says it is highly unlikely that any of Britain's elite colleges could carry out the threat deployed during the last tuition fees review to quit the state sector given what she describes as the 'insurmountable' challenges of raising enough private money in a recession: 'I don't think there is any university in the country that would be able to provide that degree of endowment.'

So for now at least, they will have to stay within the system and fight. This weekend's battle of words may be just the beginning.

'Your work ethic is what counts'
Will Walker, 22, has just graduated from Oxford Brookes University with a degree in Politics and International Relations

'I would say university is value for money. Compared with private school, tuition fees are fair, though I don't know how heavily subsidised they are. The quality of teaching varied between departments. I started off studying Economics and International Relations and changed to Politics and International Relations. A contributing factor was because of the quality of teaching on my first course; I could have been taught the subject better. I had about 12 hours' teaching time a week, though there were opportunities to meet tutors out of class. They'd expect you to do 30 hours a week, an important lesson in self-discipline.

'I felt some people could get a better result on other courses for less work. I would say it was easier to get a better result in subjects such as hospitality compared to politics. I had friends at Oxford University who would do triple or quadruple the amount of work I did. I wouldn't have coped there, I don't think.

'I've been really lucky to get a job. Your degree doesn't seem as important as I thought it was going to be. Your work ethic and ability to get along with people is what counts and university can only partly give you that.'

'Reputation is important'
About to start his final year studying history at Cambridge, 21-year-old Rob Peel of Basingstoke says he has got value for money from his degree so far

'I get five hours' teaching a week, a lot of contact time for history, and one of those hours is one-on-one supervision with a senior academic. It is an expensive system, but very beneficial.' But Rob, who wants to be a journalist, says that when it comes to comparing grades between universities, the waters get muddier.

'Theoretically grades should be comparable, but it doesn't work like that. Speaking to friends at other universities, I think it's fair to say Cambridge students have to work harder to get high grades, especially in arts subjects like mine. I attribute importance to a university's reputation. Cambridge carries a certain prestige, and those of us that get in are extremely grateful to study here. But there are other things that look good on your CV. For example, I have been editor of *Varsity*, our student newspaper, and rowed in my college boat team.' But he does not feel a rise in tuition fees is justified. 'If fees went up to a level near £7,000, people would be prohibited from going, and I don't think fees that high are value for money.'
2 August 2009

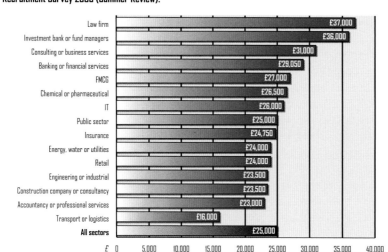

Median graduate starting salaries in 2009

The graph below shows graduate starting salaries for 2009 by employer's sectors. The information was gathered from 226 large graduate employers and was reported in the Association of Graduate Recruiters (AGR) Graduate Recruitment Survey 2009 (Summer Review).

Sector	Salary
Law firm	£37,000
Investment bank or fund managers	£36,000
Consulting or business services	£31,000
Banking or financial services	£29,050
FMCG	£27,000
Chemical or pharmaceutical	£26,500
IT	£26,000
Public sector	£25,000
Insurance	£24,750
Energy, water or utilities	£24,000
Retail	£24,000
Engineering or industrial	£23,500
Construction company or consultancy	£23,500
Accountancy or professional services	£23,000
Transport or logistics	£16,000
All sectors	£25,000

It is important to note that these salary figures are mainly from large companies and organisations who are likely to offer higher salaries. In addition, many of the vacancies are in London where salaries offered tend to be higher than in other UK regions.

Source: The AGR Graduate Recruitment Survey 2009 (Summer Review). Figures quoted on the Prospects website and accessed 15/01/10 (www.prospects.ac.uk)

Poll shows public support abolishing top-up fees

Information from Compass

On the day the Government launches its review of top-up fees, a Compass/YouGov poll shows that more than half of the public want it to look to abolish top-up fees and find alternatives. Just 12% of the public want the review to even consider increasing the cap on student top-up fees. Compass is in favour of replacing top-up fees altogether with a graduate tax, where 1% would be added to income tax for all graduates so that those who genuinely benefit from higher education would pay for the next generation.

The poll results show:

⇨ Just 12% want the review to consider increasing the cap on top-up fees.

⇨ 71% want students to be represented on top-up fees review group.

⇨ Just 30% think business should be represented on top-up fees review group.

⇨ More than half the public want student funding review group to consider abolishing top-up fees.

A clear majority of the public (71%) are also in favour of students being represented on the core review group that will decide the future of student fees, while just 30% believe business should be.

Meanwhile 81% believe the top-up fees review group should meet in public (not in private).

More than half the public want student funding review group to consider abolishing top-up fees

---

Gavin Hayes, General Secretary of Compass, said: 'It is clear that on the day the Government launch its review of student fees a clear majority of the public want top-up fees abolished altogether. The Government must now use this review to look at practical policy alternatives, a graduate tax has the real potential to widen participation whilst at the same time simplify the current archaic system. It's time the Government used a bit more imagination when it comes to the future of Higher Education.'

Neal Lawson, Chair of Compass said: 'This review will decide the future of fees paid by students and their families, and the public are overwhelmingly opposed to the intensification of the disastrous top-up fees system. There is a strong appetite to find more imaginative and popular alternatives, yet the Government is unprepared to listen and would prefer to make these decisions in private and without student representation.

'Variable tuition fees are the worst domestic policy decision of New Labour's tenure in office. The Government seem intent on a last-minute headlong rush to turn higher education into a competing market and students into consumers. It will only work for the rich who can pay the most. The rest will end up in second-class institutions, with huge debts.'
9 November 2009

⇨ The above information is reprinted with kind permission from Compass. Visit www.compassonline.org.uk for more information.

© Compass

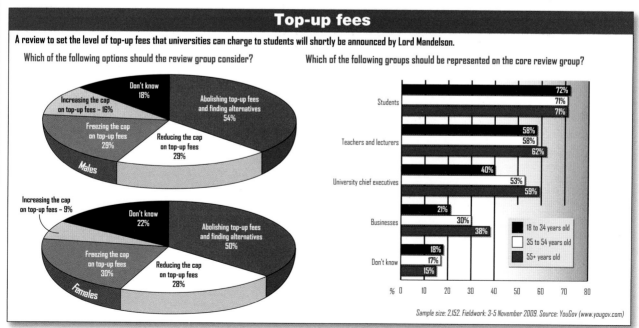

Top-up fees

A review to set the level of top-up fees that universities can charge to students will shortly be announced by Lord Mandelson.

Which of the following options should the review group consider?

Which of the following groups should be represented on the core review group?

Males
- Don't know 18%
- Increasing the cap on top-up fees – 16%
- Freezing the cap on top-up fees 29%
- Abolishing top-up fees and finding alternatives 54%
- Reducing the cap on top-up fees 29%

Females
- Increasing the cap on top-up fees – 9%
- Don't know 22%
- Freezing the cap on top-up fees 30%
- Abolishing top-up fees and finding alternatives 50%
- Reducing the cap on top-up fees 28%

Students: 72%, 71%, 71%
Teachers and lecturers: 58%, 58%, 62%
University chief executives: 40%, 53%, 59%
Businesses: 21%, 30%, 38%
Don't know: 18%, 17%, 15%

Legend:
- 18 to 34 years old
- 35 to 54 years old
- 55+ years old

% 0 10 20 30 40 50 60 70 80

Sample size: 2,152. Fieldwork: 3-5 November 2009. Source: YouGov (www.yougov.com)

Options after graduation

Options for graduates include finding a job or placement, further study at postgraduate level, setting up a business, taking a gap year or volunteering. Get planning as soon as possible – and take advantage of the advice available

Preparing for life after graduation

As you approach the end of your time in higher education, it's natural to focus more on what comes next. But there's likely to be a lot going on in your final year: lectures, essays and, of course, exams. So if you want to prepare for life as a graduate while keeping up with your studies, it pays to get organised – and to get the right advice.

Weighing up your options: work and postgraduate study

Not sure about your first step as a graduate? Talking through your options can help you come up with ideas.

Even if you've decided what you want to do, getting advice is still worthwhile. For example – if you're looking to get a particular job, will a postgraduate qualification improve your chances? Or would it be better to get some work experience?

Help is available through your university or college careers service. Subject staff can also advise on options for further study, or provide tips on where to look for careers 'leads'.

Career options and finding a job

It's best to register with the careers service as soon as possible – especially if you're looking to go straight into a job after graduation.

Volunteering after you graduate can be a great way to develop valuable skills and experience

---

As well as taking the pressure off towards the end of your final year, getting started before the rush will help you avoid missing application deadlines. You'll also benefit from early advice on planning your job search and making effective applications.

You can also get help and advice on job hunting from Jobcentre Plus.

Trying out careers while you're still at university or college

If you're curious about what it might be like to work in a particular career, there may be opportunities to find out during your time at university or college. Student societies, newspapers, radio stations, sports teams and taster courses can also help build the kind of skills and experience employers look for.

Postgraduate study

If you're considering further study, start thinking about your options as early as possible – ideally, at least 18 months before you'd be looking to start your postgraduate course.

Starting a business

Many universities offer support to students and graduates who want to start their own business. This may mean giving you the option to develop entrepreneurial skills as part of your course, or running extra-curricular advice sessions on starting a business. Some universities also provide an 'incubator' service to help graduates get their business off the ground. Ask your tutor or lecturer for details.

Another source of help and advice is the FlyingStart service, run by the National Council for Graduate Entrepreneurship.

Visit the FlyingStart website to:
⇨ use online resources, including a database of grants and funding;
⇨ network with other graduate entrepreneurs;
⇨ find out about free, one-day events to help you get started;
⇨ get details on longer-term mentoring and training programmes.

Knowledge Transfer Partnerships

A Knowledge Transfer Partnership (KTP) is a three-way project between a graduate, an organisation (such as a business, charity or public sector

WHAT'S UP?

I'M OFF TO GET A FLYING START!

Which direction should new graduates take?

body) and a university or research organisation.

As a graduate on a KTP you'll be recruited to manage a strategic project, normally lasting one to three years. Many graduates are offered a job by their KTP organisation when they complete the project.

Short KTPs

You can also apply to do shorter KTPs, lasting 10–40 weeks. These placements are mainly available in small and medium-sized enterprises (SMEs).

Volunteering

Volunteering after you graduate can be a great way to develop valuable skills and experience. Demonstrating these skills to potential employers can give you a competitive edge when it comes building your career.

There are thousands of volunteering opportunities available, so you're bound to find one that interests you. You could choose to volunteer part-time for a few days, or apply for a full-time volunteering placement in the UK or overseas.

For example, the charity Raleigh is offering bursaries to enable graduates to take part in its overseas expeditions during 2009 and 2010.

Taking a gap year

Whether you go abroad or stay in the UK, a gap year can be a good opportunity to broaden your horizons. It can also be another way of developing skills and experience to enhance your employability.

If you're after a particular gap year placement – especially one of the more popular ones – it's important to check the deadlines and make your arrangements well in advance.

⇨ The above information is reprinted with kind permission from Directgov. Visit www.direct.gov.uk for more information.

Graduate destinations

Destinations of leavers from higher education in the United Kingdom for the academic year 2007/08

Introduction

This Statistical First Release (SFR) has been produced by the Higher Education Statistics Agency (HESA), in collaboration with statisticians from the Department for Business, Innovation and Skills (BIS), the Welsh Assembly Government (WAG), the Scottish Government (SG) and the Department for Employment and Learning Northern Ireland (DEL(NI)). It has been released according to the arrangements approved by the UK Statistics Authority. It provides details of the destinations of leavers from higher education (HE) who obtained qualifications in higher education institutions (HEIs) in the United Kingdom (UK), during the academic year 2007/08. The data presented draws on the 2007/08 Destinations of Leavers from Higher Education (DLHE) record.

Key points – all UK HEIs

First degrees

⇨ In 2007/08, there were 200,090 full-time first degree graduates whose destinations were known, compared to 190,385 in 2006/07.

In 2007/08, 62% (124,065) were in employment only, 64% in 2006/07; 8% (15,265) were in a combination of work and study, 9% in 2006/07; 17% (33,170) were involved in further study only, 16% in 2006/07; and 8% (16,835) were assumed to be unemployed, 6% in 2006/07.

⇨ Of the full-time first degree graduates whose destinations were known and reported as being in employment only, 96% (118,920) were employed in the UK, the same as in 2006/07.

⇨ In 2007/08 of the full-time first degree graduates who were employed in the UK, 30% of these posts were classified as associate professional and technical occupations, 32% in 2006/07; 27% as professional occupations, the same as in 2006/07; 12% as administrative and secretarial occupations, 13% in 2006/07 and 11% as sales and customer service

occupations, 10% in 2006/07. These are the occupational groups with the highest proportions of posts.

⇨ **Subjects of study:** Unemployment rates for full-time first degree graduates whose destinations were known varied between subjects, ranging from those which have traditionally low rates of unemployment, such as medicine and dentistry 0% and Education 3%, to 12% for mass communications and documentation and 14% for computer science.

⇨ **Salary:** Of those first degree graduates (both full-time and part-time) reported as being in full-time paid employment in the UK in 2007/08, 52% disclosed their salary. The median salary reported (to the nearest £500) was £20,000 (£19,000 in 2006/07). The lower quartile was £15,000 and the upper quartile £24,000. The mean salary was £20,500 (£20,000 in 2006/07).

⇨ **Part-time:** In 2007/08, of the 21,885 part-time first degree graduates whose destinations were known, 66% (14,520) were in employment only, compared to 69% in 2006/07; 15% (3,305) were in a combination of work and study, the same as in 2006/07; 6% (1,350) were involved in further study only, the same as in 2006/07; and 5% (1,155) were assumed to be unemployed, 4% in 2006/07.

Foundation degree

⇨ In 2007/08, there were 10,150 foundation degree graduates (both full-time and part-time) whose destinations were known, compared to 8,425 in 2006/07. In 2007/08, 37% (3,715) reported their first destination as employment only, compared to 34% in 2006/07; 25% (2,580) were in a combination of work and study, compared to 26% in 2006/07; 32% (3,285) were involved in further study only, 35% in 2006/07; and 3% (300) were assumed to be unemployed, 2% in 2006/07.

Other undergraduates

⇨ In 2007/08, of the 33,920 leavers (both full-time and part-time) who obtained undergraduate diplomas and certificates (excluding foundation degrees and professional graduate certificate in education) and whose destinations were known, 61% (20,755) were in employment only, 59% in 2006/07; 16% (5,280) were in a combination of work and study, the same as in 2006/07; 16% (5,355) were in further study only, 17% in 2006/07; and 4% (1,265) were assumed to be unemployed, the same as in 2006/07.

Postgraduates

⇨ Of the 57,035 former postgraduate students (both full-time and part-time excluding postgraduate certificate in education) whose destinations were known, 75% (42,610) were in employment only, 73% in 2006/07; 10% (5,460) were in a combination of work and study, compared to 12% in 2006/07; 8% (4,405) were involved in further study only, the same as in 2006/07; and 4% (2,280) were assumed to be unemployed, 3% in 2006/07.

Gender

⇨ Overall, in 2007/08 8% of males whose destinations were known were assumed to be unemployed, compared to 5% of females; 6% and 4% respectively in 2006/07.

2 July 2009

⇨ The above information is reprinted with kind permission from the Higher Education Statistics Agency. Visit www.hesa.ac.uk for more.

© *Higher Education Statistics Agency*

Graduate earnings uncovered

New 1994 Group report

Universities are delivering on student expectations of higher graduate salaries, according to a new report by the 1994 Group of student-focused, research-intensive universities. The report compares students' employment and earning expectations when they begin university with the reality of what they achieved three-and-a-half years after graduation. It found:

⇨ More than 80% of graduates are either 'very satisfied' or 'fairly satisfied' with their careers.

⇨ Nearly two-thirds of graduates can expect to earn more than £20k a year by the time they have been in the job market for three-and-a-half years.

⇨ More than a third can expect to earn in excess of £25k.

⇨ A postgraduate qualification provides a boost to earning power.

⇨ Nearly 80% of graduates are satisfied with their choice of institution.

⇨ After three-and-a-half years, 80% of those in employment were identified as being in 'graduate level' employment.

Professor Steve Smith, Vice-Chancellor of the University of Exeter and Chair of the 1994 Group,

revealed the report's findings at a Policy Exchange Breakfast Debate this morning. He was speaking alongside Shadow Secretary of State for Innovation, University and Skills, David Willetts MP.

More than 80% of graduates are either 'very satisfied' or 'fairly satisfied' with their careers

---

Said Professor Smith: 'Students make very well-considered choices when choosing institutions and courses – and these are decisions they don't regret further down the line. There is a strong correlation between what students expect and what they get as far as employment and earnings are concerned. The vast majority of students – regardless of institution attended and subject studied – find their employment prospects and earnings potential are significantly enhanced by their experience of higher education. This underlines the importance of universities' efforts to widen participation and improve fair access.'

The 1994 Group report responds to Lord Sainsbury's call for improved information about the benefits of a degree in terms of employability and earnings premia. An increasing number of young people are seeking and obtaining a degree, and graduate employment is becoming more competitive. It is therefore important that higher education institutions are able to understand and articulate the value of a university education (although there are clearly numerous other benefits to getting a degree).

Although the vocational subjects of education and law top the table for employability, graduates from institutions across the sector are more likely to receive graduate-level jobs if they studied science and technology than arts and social sciences. Students of computer science, engineering/technology or business studies were most likely to be earning over £30k. More than 50% of UK graduates from historical and philosophical studies were earning under £20k after three-and-a-half years. Least likely to be earning under £20k were education graduates.

The data hide some differences between students from research-intensive and other institutions, and between science and technology and arts and social sciences students. The most prominent difference between the two university groupings is in science and technology, in which research-intensive graduates attract higher earnings than at other institutions. This is most marked in the £30,000 to £50,000 band in which 31.7% of graduates from research-intensive universities were placed, compared with 16% of graduates from other institutions. This trend is repeated to a less pronounced extent amongst arts and social sciences graduates of both groups.

25 November 2008

⇨ The above information is reprinted with kind permission from 1994 Group. Visit www.1994group.ac.uk for more information.

What is the average graduate starting salary?

Information on graduate salaries is available in various surveys and reports but figures tend to be different, as they are arrived at in different ways

---

1 According to latest figures released by the Higher Education Statistics Agency (HESA), the average salary for full-time first degree graduates from 2008 whose destinations were known and who were in full-time employment in the UK six months after graduating was £19,677. This figure covers graduates in all roles across the UK economy, including those occupied by graduates but which might be considered 'non-graduate', and comes from the Destinations of Leavers from Higher Education (DLHE) survey, which is the annual survey that explores graduates' destinations six months after graduation. DLHE covers all graduates from UK higher education.

2 Figures derived from the latest 2007/08 issue of *Prospects Directory* revealed that the average starting salary offered to 2008 graduates is £24,048 and the median salary* is £23,500. *Prospects Directory* is an annual graduate recruiters' directory published by Graduate Prospects and features thousands

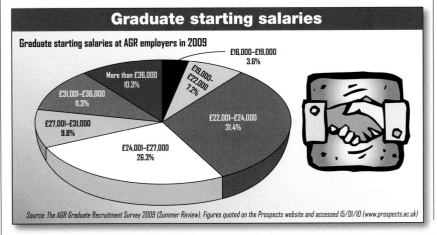

Graduate starting salaries

Graduate starting salaries at AGR employers in 2009

- £16,000–£19,000 3.6%
- £19,000–£22,000 7.2%
- More than £36,000 10.3%
- £31,001–£36,000 11.3%
- £27,001–£31,000 9.8%
- £24,001–£27,000 26.3%
- £22,001–£24,000 31.4%

Source: The AGR Graduate Recruitment Survey 2009 (Summer Review). Figures quoted on the Prospects website and accessed 15/01/10 (www.prospects.ac.uk)

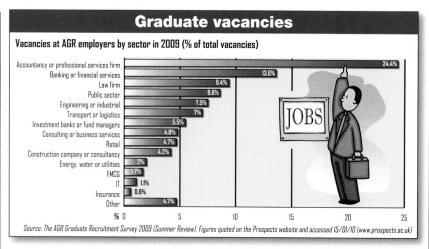

Graduate vacancies

Vacancies at AGR employers by sector in 2009 (% of total vacancies)

Sector	%
Accountancy or professional services firm	24.4%
Banking or financial services	13.6%
Law firm	9.4%
Public sector	8.6%
Engineering or industrial	7.5%
Transport or logistics	7%
Investment banks or fund managers	5.5%
Consulting or business services	4.8%
Retail	4.7%
Construction company or consultancy	4.2%
Energy, water or utilities	2%
FMCG	1.7%
IT	1.1%
Insurance	0.6%
Other	4.7%

Source: The AGR Graduate Recruitment Survey 2009 (Summer Review). Figures quoted on the Prospects website and accessed 15/01/10 (www.prospects.ac.uk)

As a result, the average salary figures from these sources are likely to be higher than the average graduate starting salaries sourced from student surveys (e.g. the figure reported by HESA), as there is a bias towards larger firms and specific graduate jobs.

The average starting salary offered to 2008 graduates is £24,048

of jobs and hundreds of employers, and the salaries are therefore derived from job advertisements. The latest 2007/08 issue is aimed at 2008 graduates. The salaries offered ranged from £14,732 to £39,000.

3 The Association of Graduate Recruiters (AGR) produced their most recent Graduate Recruitment survey in summer 2009, based on responses from 226 employers, which looks at the salaries recruiters are paying their new graduate employees. The median salary for graduates in 2009 is £25,000. This data comes from salaries paid to new employees.

It is important to note that the salary figures for the second two sources are from mainly large companies and organisations and the vacancies are aimed specifically at graduates. They are also often for formal graduate training schemes, and largely cover those sectors in which large organisations and graduate training schemes are more common. In addition, many of the vacancies are in London, where salaries offered tend to be higher than in other UK regions. These surveys are particularly useful for those graduates looking for this type of role.

A substantial number of graduates obtain posts which are not specifically targeted at degree holders, or at smaller organisations or not on formal graduate training schemes, or outside London and the south-east, and the salaries offered are likely to be closer to the figures quoted by HESA.
* *The median is the middle of a set of values.*
August 2009

⇨ The above information is reprinted with kind permission from Prospects. Visit www.prospects.ac.uk for more.
© *Prospects*

Maintaining standards in higher education

Business must do more to help maintain a world class higher education system – major new report

With the UK's higher education system facing tough choices posed by recession and competition from abroad,

business must do even more than it does to work with universities and the Government to help maintain the UK's international competitiveness, a major new report says today (Monday 25 November 2008).

The report, the culmination of a year's work by the CBI higher education task force – comprising both business and universities – also says that the rapid rise in student numbers, coupled with a severe strain on public finances, makes current public funding levels unsustainable.

The task force's report, *Stronger together – businesses and universities in turbulent times*, highlights the

vital contribution that excellence in higher education makes to business competitiveness and argues that: 'new thinking is required on the financing, structure and mission of our universities if they are to sustain and strengthen their position in a rapidly changing environment'. This means that Government, universities and students, as well as business, will have to do more if they are to maintain the strength and the quality of higher education in the UK.

The UK's higher education sector is one of the most successful in the world, and the report acknowledges that universities are a 'vital public good'.

Business needs excellent universities to produce the graduates, postgraduates, research and innovation that are required to drive economic growth and prosperity.

The UK compares quite favourably with similar countries on how many young people go to university, and undergraduate numbers have risen by 35 per cent since 1997. However, the proportion of UK graduates taking science, technology, engineering and maths (STEM) degrees has declined by 20 per cent since 1999–2000, and the CBI wants to see more young people continue with these subjects after the age of 16.

Sam Laidlaw, Chairman of the CBI HE taskforce and CEO of Centrica, said:

'The UK has a world-class higher education sector. But it faces some urgent challenges including the changing needs of business, intensifying international competition, and constrained public sector funding. Universities and Government cannot deliver a world-class service alone.

'Effective collaboration between the higher education sector, business and Government will be critical to the UK's economic recovery and sustainable international competitiveness. Bus-iness must also make a sustained effort in supporting higher education. To this end, I am pleased that as a task force we have made a strong commitment to provide the support needed to help students build the employability and technical skills that are so important.'

The report proposes that more businesses should work with universities to:
⇨ Sponsor students studying subjects relevant to business, such as science and technology.
⇨ Provide financial support to new graduates, through bonuses when they sign on with the firm.
⇨ Offer more opportunities for internships, placements, work experience or projects.
⇨ View working with universities as part of core innovation activity.

Richard Lambert, CBI director-general, said:

'Maintaining a world-class higher education system is vital to the UK's future competitiveness, and we should sustain current levels of investment in teaching and research, which are low by international standards. Strong leadership is also needed to minimise the risk of long-term decline.

'Business should engage more with universities, both financially and intellectually. More firms should help design and pay for courses for the benefit of the current and future workforce, and more firms should offer students practical work experience.

'In return for this extra investment of time and money, business will want to see more emphasis given to certain subjects, such as science, technology, engineering and maths. Languages are also seen to be important, and the task force argues that more should be done to prepare students for the world of work, and teach them the generic skills that will help smooth their pathway into employment.'

The expansion of higher education and the state of public finances is putting an increasing strain on resources. The Government has already asked universities in England to make savings of £180 million between 2009 and 2011, and many are budgeting for cuts between 10 to 20 per cent.

The expansion of higher education and the state of public finances is putting an increasing strain on resources

---

To preserve the quality of university teaching and research, the report warns that if cuts have to be made, they should be focused on what, by international standards, are generous levels of funding for student support and recommends that the Government temporarily drops its target of 50 per cent of 18- to 30-year-olds participating in higher education.

Mr Lambert added: 'The economic downturn makes cuts to public funding for higher education inevitable, so new sources of funding have to be found. Universities and business must work together to preserve the quality of teaching and research, waste in the higher education system must be cut, with universities sharing more of their services and consolidating to make efficiencies.

'On funding, our task force considered – and rejected – three options open to the Government: cutting research funding, slashing teaching budgets and reducing student numbers. Instead, we say that savings should come from the student support system. Of course, it's never easy to ask students to pay more, but the UK's student support is on a par with some of the most generous in the world, and the priority must be to preserve quality as

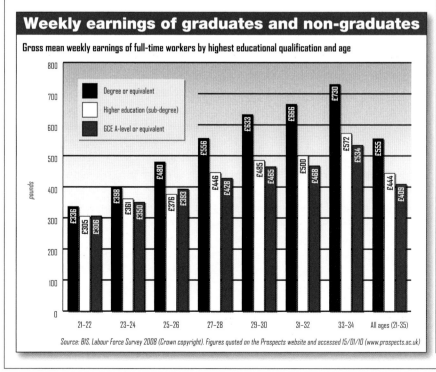

Weekly earnings of graduates and non-graduates

Gross mean weekly earnings of full-time workers by highest educational qualification and age

Degree or equivalent
Higher education (sub-degree)
GCE A-level or equivalent

21–22: £336, £305, £306
23–24: £388, £361, £350
25–26: £480, £376, £393
27–28: £556, £446, £428
29–30: £633, £485, £465
31–32: £666, £500, £468
33–34: £730, £572, £534
All ages (21–35): £555, £444, £409

Source: BIS. Labour Force Survey 2008 (Crown copyright). Figures quoted on the Prospects website and accessed 15/01/10 (www.prospects.ac.uk)

well as assisting those unable to pay to ensure that higher education remains open to all.'

The report argues that:

⇨ The Government's target for 50 per cent of 18 to 30-year-olds to participate in higher education should be dropped for the time being. Given financial pressures, the focus should be on quality not quantity. Following the surge in numbers over recent decades, the UK compares pretty well with similar countries and the priority must be on continuing to raise the performance at the school level.

⇨ Tuition fee loans should be provided at the Government's cost of borrowing. This should be phased in over a three-year period to avoid impacting on current students, and would deliver £1.4 billion savings per year.

⇨ Maintenance grants should be focused on those most in need, reversing the Government's

recent changes and returning support to 2006-07 income thresholds. Research shows the main barrier to university is attainment prior to university and that student applications have not increased as a result of the rise in income thresholds implemented in 2007-08, so it is unlikely this change would have an adverse impact on applications. It will be increasingly important for universities, with the support of business, to provide the extra bursaries that will be needed to ensure that higher education remains open to all.

⇨ An increase in fees appears inevitable. With the forthcoming review of tuition fees, likely to be up and running by the end of the year, the choice is between finding new money to put into the system or seeing student numbers decline. Universities UK has calculated that increasing the cap

to £5,000 from 2012 in England would deliver an annual increase in income for universities of £1.25 billion from 2014, without leading to a decline in student demand.

The report contains a number of challenges to the universities. It argues they should focus on their strengths, and become more specialised, but also more productive by sharing more resources. The way teaching is funded also needs to change – to give students more opportunities for work experience during their degree, encourage new and innovative teaching methods and help universities expand numbers for subjects, where there is demand, within overall public funding limits.

21 September 2009

⇨ The above information is reprinted with kind permission from CBI. Visit www.cbi.org.uk for more information.

© CBI

Graduates' outlook bleak

Major new student survey shows only a third of this year's finalists expect to find a graduate job after university

Results of one of the largest independent surveys of final-year university students ever conducted in the UK – to be published on Wednesday 29 April – shows that just 36% of those finishing undergraduate degrees this summer expect to find a graduate job after university and that confidence in the graduate employment market has slumped to a 15-year low.

The UK Graduate Careers Survey 2009, conducted by the student & graduate market research company, High Fliers Research Ltd, is based on face-to-face interviews with 16,357 final-year students completed last month. This sample equates to a fifth of the finalists due to graduate this year from the 30 universities included in the 2009 survey.

The research reveals that the number of finalists from the 'Class of 2009' who have secured a definite job offer during the annual 'milkround' recruitment process has dropped

by a third this year, compared with 2008. Half of student job hunters fear that even if they do find a graduate position, their job offer may be withdrawn before they begin work or that they will be made redundant during their first year in employment.

The survey also shows a dramatic fall in applications for graduate jobs in banking, finance and property this

year. Instead, more university leavers have applied to work in the public sector, teaching, engineering, the charity or voluntary sector and the Armed Forces. One in six job hunters confirmed that they had deliberately targeted employers that appeared to offer the best job security, rather than generous graduate salaries or high quality training and development.

The key findings from *The UK*

Graduate Careers Survey 2009 about the 'Class of 2009' are:

⇨ Just 36% of current final-year students believe they will either start a graduate job or be looking for a graduate job after leaving university this summer, 26% plan to remain at university to study for a postgraduate course, 8% expect to take temporary or voluntary work, 17% are preparing to take time off or go travelling, but 12% of finalists have yet to decide what to do next.

⇨ Students' confidence in the graduate job market is at an all-time low since the survey was launched in 1995, with a record 52% of university leavers describing prospects for new graduates as very limited.

⇨ The volume of job applications made by final-year students has increased noticeably this year, particularly in the early months of the recruitment season. But despite this, the number of finalists who have received a graduate job offer has fallen by a third compared with 2008.

⇨ A third of finalists looking for work said that, in the current economic climate, they would have to accept any job they were offered. A sixth admitted that the scarcity of graduate jobs has meant they've had to apply to employers that they weren't really interested in.

⇨ 42% of student job hunters fear that even if they do manage to land a graduate job, the offer may be cancelled by employers before they start work. 48% are concerned they may be made redundant within their first 12 months.

⇨ More finalists made applications for accountancy positions in the early months of the graduate recruitment season than any other career area, but overall the most popular destinations for the 'Class of 2009' are careers in teaching, media and marketing. This is the first time that teaching has been the top destination for university-leavers.

⇨ The number of students applying to investment banks – the second most popular destination for new graduates in 2008 – has dropped by a third this year and there has been less interest in other parts of the financial sector. Applications for jobs in property have also fallen sharply.

⇨ Applications to engineering employers and public sector organisations increased by a sixth and for the first time in nine years, more finalists have applied for IT positions.

⇨ Expected starting salaries have dipped a little this year to an average of £22,300, making this the only year that expectations have not increased since the survey was first conducted in 1995. More than a third of finalists believe that employers will cut their starting salaries this year.

A third of finalists looking for work said that, in the current economic climate, they would have to accept any job they were offered

---

⇨ Graduates from the 'Class of 2009' expect to owe an average of £15,700, up more than a third from the average debt of £11,600 in 2008, largely because of the introduction of higher tuition fees for undergraduates at English universities in 2006.

⇨ Local university careers services continue to be an important focal point for job hunting and careers activities on campus, and their facilities were used by 84% of final-year students in 2008–09 – either in person, online or via a careers module within their degree course.

⇨ Despite their concern about the worsening employment prospects, more than 90% of final-year students said they had enjoyed being at university and would recommend it to others. Fewer than one in seven said they would not have come to university if they'd known how tough the graduate job market was going to be.

Managing director of High Fliers Research Martin Birchall commented:

'Our latest survey shows that final-year students due to leave UK universities this summer are gloomy and frustrated about their employment prospects. Students are all too aware that a significant number of employers have cut their graduate recruitment programmes this year or are delaying taking on new trainees until the economic situation improves. Although many students began their job search earlier than usual and made an increased number of applications to employers, noticeably fewer have been successful in securing a graduate position than last year.

'Having invested an average of £15,000 on their degrees, tens of thousands of finalists are now set to leave university without a job offer and feel they have little prospect of finding work in the immediate future. There is widespread concern too that employers may withdraw previously-made job offers or make new graduates redundant during their first year in work.'
29 April 2009

⇨ The above information is reprinted with kind permission from High Fliers. Visit www.highfliers.co.uk for more information.

© *High Fliers*

Although there are more graduates year on year, the economic crisis means there are fewer graduate jobs to go around

Middle-class grip on professions 'must end'

Too few working-class students become doctors and lawyers, according to Downing Street, which wants to consign the old-boy network to history

By Gaby Hinsliff,
political editor

She was doubtless just as nervous as any other student on work experience, but the sober-suited blonde spotted walking through Lincoln's Inn Fields, headquarters of the British legal establishment, just before Christmas was not just any old intern.

And the role taken by Chelsy Davy, Prince Harry's girlfriend, at Farrer & Co – solicitors to the Queen – was not just any old placement. The next day's newspapers pondered uncharitably how many Leeds University students would have got the same break.

Davy might well, of course, have owed her luck purely to her legal skills, but the cosy networks helping many children of the professional middle classes into successful careers – the summer job in the City, the internship that is never openly advertised, the unpaid gofer job in the theatre eased by parental subsidy – are now coming under scrutiny.

A review of barriers to working-class entry to the professions, led by former cabinet minister Alan Milburn, will investigate not just visible causes of social inequality – children from the highest socio-economic group are nearly three times more likely than those from the lowest to get good GCSEs, and six times more likely to go to university – but more insidious factors. Its conclusions will feed into a white paper on social mobility being launched this week by Cabinet Office minister Liam Byrne.

Its timing during a recession is provocative, but senior Labour figures have long wrestled with this dilemma. Last summer the then arts minister Margaret Hodge began privately arguing for Government assistance for poorer children breaking into the arts, amid fears that creative careers were too often reserved for those whose families could support them while they worked unpaid.

Discrimination at the bar was raised nearly a decade ago by Euan Blair's mother, Cherie Booth, a self-confessed 'working-class scouser' turned QC who denounced the funding of pupillages as a 'scandal' discriminating against poorer applicants. Milburn, brought up on a council estate by his single mother, has long been interested in the issue.

Nonetheless, invoking the emotive issue of class just as rising unemployment inflames resentment of the rich will arouse suspicion. Downing Street has been poring over focus group findings suggesting that their 'do nothing' charge against the Tories was reviving forgotten perceptions of the Conservatives as unsympathetic to the poor during the last recession – undermining Cameron's portrayal of his party as modern and compassionate.

> Children from the highest socio-economic group are nearly three times more likely than those from the lowest to get good GCSEs, and six times more likely to go to university

Aides believe that last week's promise to cut taxes for savers worried about low returns on their nest eggs opens Cameron to charges of defending a wealthy elite. 'We didn't even set them a trap,' says one Downing Street aide, 'but they've walked into it.'

Yet class politics has pitfalls too, as Gordon Brown found when he entered the row over Laura Spence, a state school pupil refused a place to study medicine at Oxford University despite excellent predicted grades, triggering a national debate over whether top jobs were still shrouded in old-fashioned snobbery.

That row blurred some awkward facts: some of the candidates who beat Spence had state school backgrounds,

YES, I'M A 'WORKING CLASS' LAD...
THAT MEANS **I'LL WORK!**

while she herself later said: 'I don't feel being from a comprehensive mattered in my case.' Eight years on, only 10% of Oxbridge students come from working-class families. Can yet another review really break down such entrenched social divides?

Sitting on the shelf behind Liam Byrne in his constituency office, in the run-down Birmingham suburb of Hodge Hill, is a brightly wrapped box labelled 'Time Capsule 2020'. It contains a bundle of carefully coloured-in sheets of paper detailing the future dreams of a group of local 11-year-olds.

There are a few who want to be footballers and beauticians when they grow up, but most aspire to solidly middle-class professions. They want to be doctors, teachers and lawyers. But their tragedy is that, unless something fundamental changes, too few will make it: Hodge Hill is in the bottom 5% of the country for sending children to university, and has the fourth highest unemployment rate. So what happens between 11 and 18 to crush such dreams of a life very different from their parents'?

Byrne should know: his first job on leaving his Essex comprehensive was in McDonald's, yet he went on to university and an international career in management consultancy before entering politics. Why did he succeed where others failed? 'I had parents who loved me and pushed me and picked me up when I got things wrong.'

The paper that Byrne is launching this week will argue that there is no one solution to unlocking social mobility: rather, a constant process of levelling the playing field at all stages in life. 'The evidence says that there isn't a silver bullet, there's no one thing you can do to boost social mobility: you have got to act at every stage in someone's life,' he says.

Byrne argues that political differences over coping with recession have opened an argument about privilege and how it passes between generations. 'I'm not advocating class war: I am arguing for a battle for the majority on behalf of the majority. Cameron has revealed that not only is he not a man for the majority, he's not a man for the middle classes

either. When you look at his [savings] tax policies they don't touch 60% of pensioners.'

He argues that Cameron may be good at cultivating an everyman image 'about what tea he drinks and what kind of a kettle he would buy' but his party is reverting to type in arguing against greater investment in public services. Ministers will argue this week that such spending will create jobs and so increase 'room at the top' in professional and managerial careers for poorer children when the upturn comes.

Only 10% of Oxbridge students come from working-class families

The Tories, who published their own social mobility paper recently, will fight back by focusing on school reforms including a proposed 'pupil premium' in spending on poor students, encouraging schools to nurture them. The shadow education secretary, Michael Gove, the adopted son of a fish merchant, has noted that, of the 13,500 children who got three As at A-level last year, only 189 were on free school meals.

Both sides agree the golden age of social mobility was the 1950s, when the birth of the welfare state and growth in professional jobs swelled the middle classes: almost 40% of those born to fathers in the lowest income group in 1958 advanced into the top two income groups. By 1970, only 33% were moving up: rates have remained broadly static since.

But amid new global competition for jobs, can the logjam at the top of British society be unblocked without a painful readjustment for the middle classes?

Brown will argue this week that a billion new skilled jobs will be created worldwide over the next decade, presenting opportunities for a 1950s-style explosion of professional positions. The strategy unit report also suggests that upskilling could turn previously menial jobs into real careers: childcare could evolve into a teaching-style profession.

But first Britain must survive a recession forecast to hit the middle classes hard. Competition for places in the best state schools, the first rung on the ladder, will intensify as parents withdraw from unaffordable private education: with rising numbers of children getting degrees, formal qualifications may start to matter less than the informal networks used so well by the middle classes.

Gove argues that the recession may help break up cosy old-boy networks: 'If you have people who have acquired jobs on the basis of connections but whose ability isn't strong then they are the first that are likely to be shed.' However, he adds, middle-class children are also more likely to have gained the hard qualifications employers will now be looking for.

Byrne admits that it is impossible to stop middle-class parents playing the system, but insists it is a 'classic liberal error' to assume they have to suffer in order to give others a fair chance.

'We have got to create more room at the top again, by bringing to Britain the jobs that will be created around the world,' he says.

Nonetheless, this week's proposals are likely to bring calls from the Labour left for more radical assaults on privilege. The children of Hodge Hill may still have a mountain to climb.

11 January 2009

KEY FACTS

⇨ There are currently over two million higher education students in the UK. Higher education courses are offered at around 130 universities and higher education colleges, and many further education colleges. (page 1)

⇨ The National Student Survey shows that the overall satisfaction rate for students studying higher education in England remains high: 81 per cent said that they are satisfied with their course. (page 4)

⇨ Around one in 12 students requests counselling for a mental health problem during their time at university. Two-thirds of them are women. (page 8)

⇨ Student life can seem to revolve around alcohol, with the student bar and local pubs often the centre of the college social scene. Drinking in moderation is an enjoyable and usually harmless feature of student life. Getting drunk regularly can have potentially serious physical, social and academic effects. Even drinking to excess just occasionally can be damaging. (page 9)

⇨ The UK's largest survey of student finance, published on Push.co.uk, reveals that students who started at university in 2008 can expect to owe nearly £21,200 by the time they leave, and new students should reckon on at least £2,000 more than that. (page 12)

⇨ More than half of students surveyed by Push are in commercial debt, and two-thirds are in debt to friends and family. (page 13)

⇨ The higher education participation rate for women is now 49.2% whereas it is just 37.8% for men. Women have nearly reached the Government's 50% target while men have a long way to go. (page 14)

⇨ Over 50 per cent of young people from every social class say they want to go to university. (page 15)

⇨ The university drop-out rate is 22 per cent. (page 16)

⇨ £19,000 is the median starting salary for a new graduate in full-time employment. (page 17)

⇨ Modern universities have a more diverse student profile, including a higher proportion of black, Asian, female and older students compared to the average for all UK universities. (page 18)

⇨ Thousands of state school pupils are not applying to the most selective university degree courses despite having the A-levels to secure a place, new research shows. (page 19)

⇨ In 1450, there were three universities in Britain: Oxford, Cambridge and St Andrews. Today there are 169 higher education institutions, of which 109 are universities. (page 21)

⇨ Half of state school pupils do not think that they will be better off financially by going to certain universities over others, and teachers in the maintained sector are reluctant to discuss the different status of universities, suggest two new pieces of research commissioned by the Sutton Trust. (page 21)

⇨ More than 70 per cent of Oxford applicants are required to sit a pre-interview entrance exam in subjects such as history, English, languages, mathematics and science this term [Autumn 2009], compared with 50 per cent just two years ago. (page 23)

⇨ Secondary school teachers in England and Wales seriously underestimate the proportion of state school students at Oxford and Cambridge universities, according to an Ipsos MORI survey of nearly 500 teachers published by the Sutton Trust. (page 24)

⇨ 54% of men and 50% of women surveyed thought that the review of top-up fees led by Lord Mandelson should consider abolishing the fees and finding alternatives. (page 29)

⇨ In 2007/08, there were 200,090 full-time first degree graduates whose destinations were known, compared to 190,385 in 2006/07. In 2007/08, 62% (124,065) were in employment only, 64% in 2006/07; 8% (15,265) were in a combination of work and study, 9% in 2006/07; 17% (33,170) were involved in further study only, 16% in 2006/07; and 8% (16,835) were assumed to be unemployed, 6% in 2006/07. (page 31)

⇨ More than 80% of graduates are either 'very satisfied' or 'fairly satisfied' with their careers. (page 32)

⇨ Nearly two-thirds of graduates can expect to earn more than £20k a year by the time they have been in the job market for three-and-a-half years. (page 32)

⇨ According to latest figures released by the Higher Education Statistics Agency (HESA), the average salary for full-time first degree graduates from 2008 whose destinations were known and who were in full-time employment in the UK six months after graduating was £19,677. (page 33)

⇨ Undergraduate numbers have risen by 35 per cent since 1997. (page 35)

GLOSSARY

A-levels
This stands for Advanced level. These are qualifications usually taken by students aged 16 to 18 at schools and sixth-form colleges, although they can be taken at any time by school leavers at local colleges or through distance learning. They provide an accepted route to degree courses and university and usually take two years to complete.

Degree
An honours degree is the most common qualification awarded on graduation from university. It is graded according to classification: first class (a 'first'), upper second class (2:1), lower second class (2:2), third class (a 'third') and fail.

Further education (FE)
Post-16 education, usually provided by a sixth form or FE college offering A-levels and vocational courses.

Gap year
A year away from study or full-time employment, usually taken before starting university or after graduating. Gap years can help students to broaden their horizons through travel or volunteering.

Graduate
Someone who has studied for and been awarded a degree.

Halls of residence
Most new students live in accommodation provided by the university, called halls of residence. However, there are alternatives, such as 'living out' (renting privately with a group of housemates) or living at home if you are studying nearby.

Higher education (HE)
Post-18 education, usually provided by a university and leading to the award of a degree or postgraduate qualification. There are currently over two million higher education students in the UK.

Oxbridge
A portmanteau word referring to the two most prestigious universities in the UK, Oxford and Cambridge.

Polytechnic
Between the 1960s and 1992, institutions known as polytechnics existed across England, Wales and Northern Ireland. Their aim was to teach both academic and vocational subjects, and they could award qualifications equivalent to a university degree. In 1992, polytechnics were granted the right to become fully-fledged universities. They are often referred to as the 'new universities', 'modern universities', or, less formally, 'ex-polys'.

Postgraduate
A postgraduate is a student who has completed a degree and gone on to further academic study, such as a PhD or Master's course.

Social mobility
The ability of an individual to move around within the class system. In the past, social mobility was an almost unheard-of concept, whereas today we would think little of the daughter of a builder growing up to become an accountant, or a doctor's son forgoing higher education and training as a plumber. However, there are worries that social mobility in the UK has slowed since the seventies and may come to a halt.

State school
A school which is funded and run by the Government, at no cost to the pupils. An independent school, on the other hand, is one which is privately run and which pupils pay a fee to attend. These are sometimes known as 'private schools' or 'public schools'.

Student debt
A higher education student can apply for a student loan from the government, which they begin paying back monthly after graduation once they are earning a certain salary. They may also incur additional debts such as overdrafts while at university. There are concerns that student debt is rising to unmanageable levels: recent research from Push suggests that students beginning university in 2009 can expect to owe £23,500 by the time they graduate.

Top-up fees
The Government gives universities a capped fee – £3,225 per student, but courses cost about four times that figure to run. Top-up fees exist to 'top up' the Government's contribution to pay for the course. They were introduced in the academic year 2006-07 and vary by institution. Top-up fees have been highly controversial.

Undergraduate
An undergraduate is a term applied to a student studying towards a first degree but who has not yet graduated.

Vocational
A qualification which is relevant to a particular career and can be expected to provide a route into that career. Examples are qualifications in accountancy or journalism. This differs from an academic qualification, which focuses on a particular academic subject such as History or Maths.

INDEX

Additional Resources

Other Issues titles

If you are interested in researching further some of the issues raised in *Student Matters*, you may like to read the following titles in the **Issues** series:

⇨ Vol. 183 *Work and Employment* (ISBN 978 1 86168 524 7)

⇨ Vol. 180 *Money and Finances* (ISBN 978 1 86168 504 9)

⇨ Vol. 176 *Health Issues for Young People* (ISBN 978 1 86168 500 1)

⇨ Vol. 175 *Citizenship and Participation* (ISBN 978 1 86168 489 9)

⇨ Vol. 154 *The Gender Gap* (ISBN 978 1 86168 441 7)

⇨ Vol. 149 *A Classless Society?* (ISBN 978 1 86168 422 6)

⇨ Vol. 139 *The Education Problem* (ISBN 978 1 86168 391 5)

For more information about these titles, visit our website at www.independence.co.uk/publicationslist

Useful organisations

You may find the websites of the following organisations useful for further research:

⇨ **Compass:** www.compassonline.org.uk

⇨ **Dept. for Business, Innovation and Skills:** www.bis.gov.uk

⇨ **Directgov:** www.direct.gov.uk

⇨ **HEFCE:** www.hefce.ac.uk

⇨ **HEPI:** www.hepi.ac.uk

⇨ **HESA:** www.hesa.ac.uk

⇨ **million+:** www.millionplus.ac.uk

⇨ **NUS:** www.nus.org.uk

⇨ **Prospects:** www.prospects.ac.uk

⇨ **Push:** www.push.co.uk

⇨ **Sutton Trust:** www.suttontrust.com

FOR MORE BOOK INFORMATION, VISIT OUR WEBSITE...

www.independence.co.uk

Information available online includes:

- ✓ **Detailed descriptions of titles**
- ✓ **Tables of contents**
- ✓ **Facts and figures**
- ✓ **Online ordering facilities**
- ✓ **Log-in page for *Issues Online* (an Internet resource available free to all Firm Order *Issues* subscribers – ask your librarian to find out if this service is available to you)**

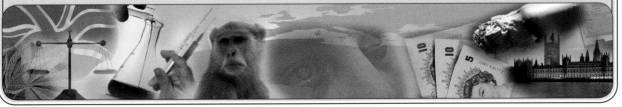

ACKNOWLEDGEMENTS

The publisher is grateful for permission to reproduce the following material.

While every care has been taken to trace and acknowledge copyright, the publisher tenders its apology for any accidental infringement or where copyright has proved untraceable. The publisher would be pleased to come to a suitable arrangement in any such case with the rightful owner.

Chapter One: Student Issues

The benefits of higher education, © Crown copyright is reproduced with the permission of Her Majesty's Stationery Office, *Going to university,* © TheSite.org, *What is higher education really like?,* © Crown copyright is reproduced with the permission of Her Majesty's Stationery Office, *High levels of satisfaction among students,* © HEFCE, *Choosing a course,* © InterStudent, *Joining clubs and societies,* © NUS, *Student housing: the basics,* © need2know, *Student mental health,* © NHS Choices, *Smoking, alcohol, drugs,* © NHS Choices, *Student drinking problems,* © Linwood Group, *Student costs breakdown,* © TheSite.org, *Push releases figures for 2009 student debt survey,* © Push, *Survey puts spotlight on commercial debt,* © NUS, *Gender and higher education,* © HEPI.

Chapter Two: University Standards

Does a degree really set you up for life?, © Guardian Newspapers Ltd 2010, *Boosting social mobility,* © million+, *State school pupils shun top degree courses,* © Sutton Trust, *New universities to revert to old polytechnic role,* © Times Newspapers Ltd, *Higher education and earning power,* © Sutton Trust, *Oxbridge introduce new entrance tests,* © Telegraph Group Limited, London 2010, *Teachers show alarming Oxbridge misconceptions,* © Sutton Trust, *Mandelson outlines the future of higher education,* © Crown copyright is reproduced with the permission of Her Majesty's Stationery Office, *How do we tell the good universities from the bad?,* © Guardian Newspapers Ltd 2010, *Poll shows public support abolishing top-up fees,* © Compass.

Chapter Three: Graduate Prospects

Options after graduation, © Crown copyright is reproduced with the permission of Her Majesty's Stationery Office, *Graduate destinations,* © Higher Education Statistics Agency, *Graduate earnings uncovered,* © 1994 Group, *What is the average graduate starting salary?,* © Prospects, *Maintaining standards in higher education,* © CBI, *Graduates' outlook bleak,* © High Fliers, *Middle-class grip on professions 'must end',* © Guardian Newspapers Ltd 2010.

Photographs

Stock Xchng: pages 8, 13a (Sanja Gjenero); 11 (Carl Silver); 13b (mihow); 15 (Mary Gober); 17 (Sergio Roberto Bichara); 20 (Patrick Leahy); 27 (Sara Haj-Hassan); 31 (Jan Kratena); 32 (Kat Jackson); 34 (Yaroslav B); 37 (B S K).

Illustrations

Pages 1, 10, 30, 38: Don Hatcher; pages 2, 23, 31: Angelo Madrid; pages 5, 22, 36: Simon Kneebone; pages 19, 26: Bev Aisbett.

And with thanks to the team: Mary Chapman, Sandra Dennis, Claire Owen and Jan Sunderland.

Lisa Firth
Cambridge
January, 2010